DIVINE DETOURS

LOVE BOLDLY > LIVE FEARLESSLY

ROGER CLEMENT

with Kayla Hollowell

Scripture Verses:

NIV Life Application Bible,
Zondervan {A part of Harper Collins Christian Publishing } (Copyright 2011)
Grand Rapids, MI

NKJV, Thomas Nelson Publishers, (Copyright 1975) Grand Rapids, MI

I dedicate this book to my loving wife,

Roxanne Clement.

Thank you for being an amazing wife, mother, friend, encourager, and woman with a heart for God.

Your loving choices live on in our hearts and will never be forgotten.

ACKNOWLEDGMENTS

Without these amazing supporters, this book could not exist.

Thank you so much to Kayla Hollowell, who spent more than two years of her life recreating and writing this beautiful story.

Thank you to Bailey Gray, who took the time to collect all of my texts to Team Roxanne and put them into word format for me.

Thank you to David and Kay Chung, who spent endless hours editing and took the time to encourage me through my grief.

Thank you to Pat Brown, Sue Osmon and Abigail Skinner who contributed countless hours reading and editing.

To Matt and Kristen Kleppe and Dick and Connie Nervig, for their editing input and encouragement.

To Tracey O'Malley at Catalyst Creative Marketing Group who designed the book logo and layout.

Also, a special thank you to Team Roxanne for their endless support, encouragement and care.

And lastly, my mother, Vera Buell, for being my number one cheerleader and always believing in me.

I will be forever grateful to all of you.

NEVER SAY NEVER

Once upon a time I was confident that I would never become a divorcee, never raise a grandchild, never be like my Dad, never turn into a workaholic, never be comfortable sitting in a hospital for days on end with a sick person, and I would certainly never write a book.

In spite of my intense determination, I eventually learned that every time I used the word, "never" in a sentence, I was in for an awakening! God often does funny things with the word, "never," especially when our use of the word is motivated by fear.

Change is intimidating, but if we don't learn to choose faith over fear, we will not experience the mighty hand of God in our lives. Seeing the power of God at work is only possible when we attempt the impossible, giving Him the ultimate authority to direct every choice we make. Before we can soar on wings like eagles, we must first find the faith to jump off into the unknown, trusting God to fulfill His promises and catch us.

While we try to personify God as rational and predictable, expecting Him to work within the maps and boundaries we have established for our lives, He often guides us on alternative pathways through detours that don't seem to make sense.

Noah didn't understand why he was commanded to build an ark. Moses couldn't understand why God chose him to lead the Israelites out of Egypt. Peter, who had literally walked with Jesus for three years, didn't understand how Jesus could think he would ever deny Him. Yet, Peter did the unimaginable three times within hours of that prediction.

Through situations many believers thought they would never face, God has accomplished His glorious purpose and displayed the true depth of His love for us.

Life constantly presents us with the unexpected. Left to my own human nature, I am capable of making choices, both good and bad, that I could never have imagined. Thankfully, God has used both wise and foolish decisions I have made to teach me more about His character and the extent of His love for me. In times of triumph and times of tragedy, His kindness and compassion have never failed me.

In *Divine Detours*, you will catch a glimpse of the boundless love God has for each one of us, and how He can take our fears, failures, and sorrows and turn them into precious gifts and opportunities for growth. You will discover how an average person or family can have a lasting impact on their world, learn relationship-building principles that work for any relationship, and find positive ways to deal with the most negative circumstances of your life.

Most of all, you will see what is possible when you allow God to direct your steps and how He provides the exact amount of grace you need in your hour of need.

I never dreamed that I would return to ministry, go on a mission trip, or manage to finish this book. I was convinced that I wasn't spiritual enough, smart enough, strong enough, or capable of succeeding. But, the good news is, I don't have to be "enough."

Throughout the writing process, God has shown me how He can enable me to do whatever I need to do, provide any resource I need, and equip me to weather any storm of life. He is in charge of making this book a success and using my story to inspire change in your life.

The Bible defines wisdom as life's greatest prize, and it only comes by knowing and trusting God. Most often wisdom is manifested when God takes us to the edge of the canyon called, "never" and invites us to "Jump!"

God has charged me with the task of sharing my "jumping" experiences with you and describing how He has turned those leaps of faith into life changing lessons, astonishing blessings, and even miracles.

In this book, I disclose the most difficult detours of my life and how God has used them to help others and shape me into the man I am today.

As you read my life story, I challenge you to consider your own personal journey. I pray that you will ask the Lord to reveal how He is working in your life today.

Is there something He has called you to do? Are you stuck in a detour, unsure of your next move? I can assure you that God has a purpose for every day of your life and if you can muster the courage to "jump," you will see His marvelous plan unfold as you join Him on this great adventure called life.

May God bless you and keep you,

Roger

TABLE OF **CONTENTS**

TABLE OF CONTENTS

01 〉〉

when happily ever after
DOESN'T
HAPPEN

"We experience aloneness one of two ways.
Loneliness or Solitude.
Loneliness is a wound, something that hurts and makes us miserable.
Solitude is a gift where we discover how much we are loved by God."

- Henri J.M. Nouwen

It's a beautiful sunny day and you're driving down the highway with the cruise control set. You think to yourself, "I'm making really good time!" You're listening to your favorite music and life is good. Then suddenly, you see a sign with a flashing orange light that reads, "Slow Down. Detour Ahead." Before you know it, you're on a side road full of rush hour traffic moving at about 30 mph. You quickly go from thinking you're going to be early to being an hour late. Your face gets flushed, your heart starts pounding, your muscles tense and your frustration level goes through the roof. A detour can change a good day into a bad one in the blink of an eye, and life is fraught with detours. Everything can be running along smoothly when an unexpected detour changes your course and suddenly life seems out of control.

I have had plenty of small detours in my life, but in 2002 my life took a turn I never expected. After a heated argument with my wife the previous night, I awoke at 4 AM with severe chest pains. Our marriage had been progressively going downhill, and with each fight the stress had grown. Now, unbeknownst to me, I was only moments away from cardiac arrest.

Ignorant of the seriousness of the matter, I took a few aspirin and tried to go back to sleep. I dozed off for an hour, but then the pains became unbearable. Something was very wrong. Unsure of what to do, I went to my primary care doctor that morning to talk to him about my chest pain. He looked shocked and told me to go to the emergency room immediately. Once I arrived, they rushed me in and started doing tests. Before long the doctor appeared and told me that I had just had a heart attack, and they needed to do surgery as soon as possible. Moments later, they rushed me into surgery and placed two stents into my heart.

While in the recovery room, my cardiologist came in to let me know how the procedure went. After several questions about my stress levels before the attack, he told me that I needed to make serious changes in my life to prevent another episode. As he warned me about the devastating effects that stress can have on the heart, my mind went back over the past several months. I quickly recognized that I had experienced chest pains during every one of the arguments with my wife. I barely heard him as he prattled on about dietary and exercise plans. I had to make a change, or this cycle would never end. My body was not tolerating the increasing stress of my home life.

Later that year after another unpleasant dispute and a bout of chest pain, I couldn't take anymore. The hurt and anger inside was eating me alive and it had turned me into a walking volcano. I hated the man I had become and barely recognized myself in the mirror. Desperate for answers and in need of some peace and quiet, I grabbed my suitcase and decided to stay in a hotel for the night. I hoped that some serious time with God would help me gain a fresh perspective.

After I had settled into my room, I laid face first on the floor and prayed like I had never prayed before. With my face buried in the carpet, I told God I wouldn't get up until He told me what to do. Minutes later I heard Him chime in, "Why don't you go to the Christian Book Outlet?" Thinking that an extremely odd response, I asked a few more times. I thought surely my imagination was playing tricks on me, but after I realized God wasn't changing His answer, I reluctantly agreed to go. I had no clue what I was even looking for, but I prayed that God would guide me to exactly what I needed.

As I drove, my faith dangled by a thread. Fear had me by the throat and wasn't letting go. It was sucking the life right out of me. I cried aloud, "God, I am losing my mind. What have I done to deserve this? Where did I go wrong, Lord? What do I do now? Is this all my fault?" I expected that we would stay together until time ended or one of us died. No matter how crazy life got, I thought my marriage would be the one thing that would last. I never even considered what I would do if I was wrong. Now, I needed a miracle.

When I got to the bookstore, I sat in the parking lot and prayed again. *Please help me, God. I need You to show me what to do, because I can't do this by myself. You are my only hope.* I tried to compose myself as I walked inside. At first glance, the entire store became a fuzzy blur and only one book caught my eye. It stuck out like a neon sign, as if nothing else in the room existed. I knew that God had led me straight to it. The title was *Hurt People Hurt People* by Sandra Wilson and I was definitely hurt. After I purchased it, I went back to my hotel for the night to calm myself and concentrate on reading and praying for guidance. By the time I finished the book the next day, I had a divine peace about what I needed to do.

As I meditated on the principles in that book, it became obvious to me that something had to change drastically for my marriage to be healthy again. God showed me that I needed to remove myself from the situation in order for Him to work. Because respectful face-to-face communication had become nearly impossible, I wrote a letter to my wife stating that I was moving out. I explained that I was not leaving for another woman or because I wanted a divorce, but to allow us the space to rebuild the foundation of our marriage.

Her response told me that she might not be receptive to patching things up. Still, I wasn't going to give up easily. I assured her that I was committed to do whatever it took to get our marriage onto a healthy platform, but I would no longer live with a relationship lacking healthy love and respect. I was convinced that the only way to save my marriage was to start over at square one.

My hopes were high, but I soon found myself struggling with exactly where "square one" should be. When it came to starting over, I was pretty clueless. As I packed my things in preparation for moving out, I mulled it over. I tried to recall exactly what had brought us to such a low point. By retracing my steps, I hoped I would discover how I went wrong so we could get back on the right track, renew our commitment and finally find healing.

Sifting through my memories took me all the way back to when I was 16. I had saved enough money to buy a blue 1957 Renault and had fixed it up just as summer was coming to an end. I would strap my surfboard onto the roof and sing along.

with the Beach Boys at the top of my lungs all the way to the beach, where I spent countless hours hanging out with friends and catching waves. On Friday nights, it served as my love wagon at the drive-in movie. I thought I was living the dream.

The only problem was that I had no one special to share my dream life with. I had been on plenty of dates, but none that held my interest. More than anything, I longed to be "in love." I had seen it in movies, read about it in fairytales and heard my friends talk about how wonderful it was. I could hardly wait to fall in love, get married and live happily ever after. With someone to love and take care of, life would be a dream come true. If only it were that easy.

I was naïve and unsure of what I really wanted in a partner, other than that I wanted to have a strong physical connection. I didn't have a clue what I wanted emotionally, mentally or spiritually in a wife, so I focused on finding someone attractive who could give my ego a boost.

The summer before my sophomore year of college began, I was sure I had found the right girl for me. Suddenly the past two unproductive years of my love quest seemed worthwhile. The moment I saw her, my heart skipped a beat. She was a tall, thin, blonde beauty and I had to know who she was. I mustered up the courage to ask her out and when she said, yes, I felt like I had just won a million bucks.

I couldn't wait to sweep her off her feet. After only three or four dates, I felt sure that we were "in love." When she was with me, I was on cloud nine. Every moment we spent together, warm, fuzzy feelings and a belly full of butterflies became the norm. When she was in my arms, I felt at peace with the world. Being in love was even better than I imagined. I was instantly hooked on the feeling.

Like most dating relationships, we tried to project ourselves as healthy, successful, happy people. We avoided conversations about conflicts, weaknesses, or character.

flaws. Wanting to impress each other, we worked hard to do so, and it worked. In less than a year we were engaged.

We had a small country wedding, and as I said, "I do," visions of forever filled my mind. I pictured us owning a beautiful farm in the country. We would have our own vegetable garden, decorate our Christmas tree together with our children, and spend yearly vacations at the beach. When we retired we would have coffee together on our front porch and enjoy watching the sun come up. I could hardly wait to start my fairytale life with the woman I loved.

After our blissful four-day honeymoon, we moved to an apartment in Fayetteville because I was still in college and our country home wasn't quite in our budget yet. The first few years we were both busy with work and school. Then, our first daughter, Lynn, was born a month before I graduated, only two years after we married.

My daughter, Lynn, and me on graduation day

By the time she was a year old, life had settled into a slower routine. Because we had more time to spend together, my wife and I began to notice how different we really were.

We found ourselves struggling to connect in ways we never realized we needed to when we were dating. The reality of living together, establishing a home, and having a family brought about situations that neither of us knew how to handle. Past experiences we had neglected to discuss were greatly affecting the way we thought, prioritized and made day-to-day decisions. Neither of us had been insightful enough to deal with those issues before we wed. Those unexplored areas of each other's lives were wreaking havoc on our self-esteem, heaping hurt upon hurt. Because we tried desperately to be heard and understood, we often neglected trying to understand each other. Our need to be heard became the biggest barrier between us, and hindered our ability to respond respectfully.

After five years of wondering if our marriage would make it, life took a turn for the better when I experienced a spiritual awakening. Though we had always attended church together, neither of us had truly experienced letting Jesus be Lord of our lives. I had spent most of my time pursuing my plan for myself rather than God's plans for me. After seeking councel from my pastor about it, I asked the Lord to take over my life and prayed that my wife would soon do the same. For the first time, I began actively applying biblical principles to my life and seeking God's will for every situation I faced.

As I drew closer to the Lord, I began to realize how selfish I had been in most of my relationships, including my marriage. As a result, I invited God to teach me how to love others the way He loves them. He seemed more than happy to tackle that request. Before long He radically changed the way I handled my relationships, enriched my work and ministry, and drew our family closer than ever.

After a year, my wife noticed how drastically different I was and that it wasn't just an act. Then God answered my prayers and she asked Jesus to be Lord of her life as well. We agreed to work harder to improve our marriage and had several good years. As we prayed together daily and became very active in our church, the spiritual connection soon became our strongest link. We still struggled occasionally in the other areas, but our spiritual commitment brought a sense of strength and peace to our relationship.

Our second daughter, Casey, was born six years after Lynn. As I watched my family grow, I purposed in my heart never to be like my dad, who was often too busy for family time. Because I didn't want my daughters to feel like my work was more important than they were to me, I started making a serious effort to spend quality time with them when I was home. Unfortunately, our busy family and church life made it very easy for my wife and me to fall back into the habit of ignoring our lack of connection in the mental, emotional and eventually, the physical realm, too.

As our daughters got older and their lives became more active, the spotlight turned back on the obvious lack of connection in our marriage. When we honestly tried to deal with the mental, emotional and physical realities about each other, there were more disconnects than there were connections. I began to wonder how long our relationship could make it with only a single area of harmony.

My inability to connect the way I wanted to resulted in my feeling extremely needy and vulnerable, both emotionally and physically. I didn't know what else to do, so as a distraction from our emotional struggles, I poured myself into my work and spent even less time trying to address our issues. My wife noticed my lack of concern. In response, she distanced herself further from me as well. That created even more tension between us.

In 1989, I founded my own financial firm. Though my home situation wasn't improving, I found comfort in knowing that my business was going well. In addition to my business, I also got involved in ministry. I spoke in hundreds of churches on the subject of finances, which started taking up more of my family time. My workaholic lifestyle grew more out of control than ever and my relationships were visibly suffering the consequences. Avoiding my marital woes was like stuffing trash into a closet rather than taking it to the dumpster. The garbage between my wife and me was piling up. At any moment I feared that the enormous heap of misunderstandings and miscommunications would come tumbling down, burying me under its weight.

Though we were both unhappy and unhealthy, I stubbornly pressed on throughout the years. I had been taught that divorce was always wrong and definitely not an option for a Christian. I believed that if I worked hard enough, prayed hard enough and just hung in there, it would eventually work itself out. Yet there I was, moving into an apartment after 30 years of living in a troubled marriage. It was clear that our problems had only worsened. My heart broke as I realized that it had made me and everyone else in my home dangerously unhealthy. Denying the truth and staying busy to cope with the situation had only intensified the hurt and anger we felt towards each other.

Those realities had hit me like a ton of bricks as I read *Hurt People Hurt People* in my hotel room a few days before. The author made a statement in the book that I had never considered, but it rang so true to my heart. She said, "God does hate divorce. He said He did in the Bible, but there are some things He hates more." She covered subjects such as alcoholism, drug abuse, physical abuse, child abuse, mental illness and other dysfunctions that make a healthy relationship impossible unless the struggling individuals are willing to get help.

In my business, I had spent 14 years teaching people how to handle their finances. I met thousands of couples that were ignoring the basic principles of developing and adhering to a written spending plan in order to avoid the debt trap. No matter how sweet and sincere those people were, they were at risk for financial failure if they did not make radical changes in the way they handled their money.

Many couples experienced the blessings of making those adjustments, but others were simply not willing to make the necessary sacrifices. Those couples often had to deal with failure, not only financially, but in their marriages as well. I suddenly realized that the same principle applied to my marital struggles. If my wife and I refused to change the things that were undermining our marriage, we were also destined for failure.

With a heavy but hopeful heart, I finally got settled into my apartment and began praying that God would show us the pathway to reconciliation and restoration. Despite my fears and doubts, I was truly committed to do whatever it took. I prayed desperately that God would either show me how to fix my marriage or give me the strength and peace in my heart to let it go. I attended counseling every week and often had additional sessions with my wife. We even attended a marriage-in-crisis event that included 30 hours of group therapy, but all of those efforts proved fruitless.

As it became evident that I might become a divorced man, I considered divorce recovery classes and read several books on how to survive divorce as a believer. Ten months after we separated, my worst fears were confirmed when divorce became imminent. Separation was a major detour for me, but the threat of a pending divorce took me down yet another unexpected detour. Before I knew it, I found myself stuck in a place I never intended to visit and never thought I'd escape—loneliness.

After many years of marriage, I never imagined myself having to deal with loneliness again. Yet, after the divorce was filed, I found myself facing it on a whole new level. Not only did my marriage fall apart, but the rest of my life seemed to as well. Since I had always been told divorced people shouldn't be in ministry, I stepped out of my ministry position of 13 years and consequently lost most of my friends.

I honestly wasn't sure what to do with my situation or myself. The activities that once consumed the majority of my time no longer filled my schedule. I had more time than I knew what to do with, so I began searching for answers on how to rebuild my life.

Through books, messages and counseling, God spoke to me about the concept of solitude. I didn't understand the concept initially. Then it occurred to me that since I married at age 19, I had never really spent much time by myself. When I considered the possibility that I might be alone for a considerable amount of time, if not for the rest of my life, I felt profoundly isolated. I was thinking, *I need somebody. I can't stand the thought of being alone.*

I wasn't quite sure what to do about that, but I was determined to avoid letting my neediness lead to even bigger problems. In my daily reading I stumbled across a book that emphasized the importance of learning to be alone, realizing that I didn't need someone, and accepting that God is enough. I confess that at first I wanted to rebel. That knowledge required me to start making radical changes within myself that I wasn't sure I was prepared to make.

As I thought about my bachelor years, I realized that I had never considered that I should find happiness or contentment within my relationship with God. I spent most of my young life searching for relationships that would add purpose or pleasure to my life and very little time asking God who He wanted me to be or what He wanted me to do. I failed to consider that what I wanted for my life and in my relationships might not be what God wanted.

I highly suspected that my lack of effort to search out the will of God for my life and my romantic choices might be the reason I came to be in such a predicament. I began to wonder how much pain and confusion I could have saved myself if I had been willing to search for God's plan instead of making my own. As regret set in, I understood that my lack of effort had some pretty serious consequences for both my family and myself. I knew I could not reverse time and it would do me no good to wish that I could. Rather than drown in bitterness and defeat, I decided to let the past teach me a lesson.

Since I had previously spent so little time alone, I soon discovered that loneliness is often accompanied by fear and desperation. At times I panicked as I realized how easy it could be for a person to gravitate to the first potential relationship that came along. During those moments, I just wanted temporary relief from all the loneliness. However, I knew that God was saying, "Roger, until you learn to be alone and realize that you can be happy, content and fulfilled within yourself, you will not be a good partner for anyone. Needy people don't make healthy partners." Bewildered and not fully convinced, I resolved to embrace solitude. I resisted the urge to seek short term relief from being alone and concentrated on my own mental,

>> **Needy people do not make healthy partners.**

emotional and spiritual well being. Although it was the most difficult time in my life, I slowly developed an amazing awareness of God's presence and peace each step of the way.

Eight months later, I could honestly say that I knew God and myself a whole lot better. I was confident that I had given my best in attempting to restore my marriage and had successfully avoided any other relationships. Not only had I accepted solitude, I had come to appreciate and even enjoy it. I began to see things that I had never noticed before, such as the beauty of the world around me and the simple joy of having a stressfree place to live and rest.

During that time, I also acknowledged the full effect of my past mistakes. I knew I had to live differently from that point on if I was going to pull my life back together. I had spent too many years avoiding my problems rather than facing them, and I was more than ready to start looking for healthier solutions.

Sins, failures and mistakes are a very painful part of life, no one is perfect enough to avoid them. I often wished I never had to face them, yet, if I allowed them to be my teachers, they would eventually become stepping stones to bigger successes than I would have ever experienced otherwise. My marriage might be considered the biggest failure of my life to date, but if I applied what I learned through the experience, I knew I would have a much better chance at avoiding a future repeat.

The definition of insanity is often stated as "doing the same things over and over again expecting different results." I had quoted that proverb to many of my clients and it occurred to me that I honestly needed to take my own advice. I definitely did not want to walk the path of insanity. I determined to do the right things mentally, spiritually, emotionally and physically to avoid future failures and continue the healing process. I was learning what doing the right things entailed, but I had a lot of growing ahead of me to fulfill that commitment.

POINTS2PONDER
TROUBLED relationships ▸ ≫

1: Describe a time when an important relationship in your life became troubled or ended unexpectedly. What fears and struggles did it uncover?

_____

_____

_____

_____

2: If your last relationship ended badly, what choices did you make that contributed to the breakdown of the relationship? What could you do differently in the future?

_____

_____

_____

_____

3: In what ways can times of solitude with God be nurturing?

_____

_____

_____

_____

4: Identify a negative element in one of your current relationships and list some ways you could promote healthy change in that relationship.

_____

_____

_____

_____

5: What has been your biggest failure to date and what has it taught you?

_____

_____

_____

_____

6: Do you believe separating temporarily might allow room for healing and growth and possibly save a troubled relationship? Why or why not?

_____

_____

_____

_____

02

an
UNHAPPY
ENDING

"Being divorced is like being hit by a Mack Truck. If you live through it, you start looking to the right and to the left."

- Jean Kerr

The first few miles of a detour are usually pretty rough. Traffic moves at a snail's pace and time seems to pass just as slowly. If the detour goes on long enough, I usually grow accustomed to it and learn to relax again. Being separated from my spouse of 30 years was a similar adjustment in pace. It took almost six months for me to get past the random moments of panic and fear while learning how to take care of myself again.

Though divorce papers had been filed, we hadn't signed them yet, so in my heart I chose to hold on to the dwindling chance of reconciliation. It was my honest hope that by becoming a healthier man I might someday be able to make my marriage healthy again. For nine months I tried everything I could think of to restore our love. I read at least 35 self-help books and worked hard on self discovery exercises assigned by my counselor. I never missed a session. However, when my wife started leaving counseling in the middle of our sessions, I realized that she had simply lost the will to work it out. I had failed her for too long.

When the divorce papers were served, an entirely new reality hit me. It became obvious that our relationship was not going to get better and that it could easily turn ugly. The shame and guilt in my heart was almost unbearable. Somehow I had to come to grips with the fact that my family was permanently broken, and the person I thought I would spend the rest of my life with was gone. I had no idea what to do with the rest of my life and that uncertainty was unnerving.

Regardless of which side you're on, divorce is a painful experience. Lawyers and judges took charge of my life and scrutinized every word I said, everything I did and every penny I spent. It felt like someone had taken a load of my dirty laundry and hung it in my front yard for all to see.

If you have children of any age, divorce often causes them anguish. I struggled to find ways to help my adult kids through the process, but I soon found that much of what I said made it more difficult rather than making it easier. For them, no offense was serious enough to warrant dividing our family.

I could see the look of disappointment in their eyes, which told me that they had lost their trust in me. I was ashamed of myself every time I looked at them.

To make matters worse, people outside my family were also hurt over the situation. I was shocked when most of my friends stopped talking to me. My four closest friends even made a special trip to my apartment just to chew me out and didn't speak to me again after that talk. They held me solely responsible for the dissolution of my marriage. Even if I were to blame, I desperately needed their support and friendship. I'm still not sure what good they thought it would do to scold me rather than pray for me and offer wise counsel. Naturally, I felt betrayed.

I thought I could surely seek refuge within my church family. However, I was absolutely bewildered on my first Sunday at church after people learned of my pending divorce. Since I had counseled so many people throughout my ministry, I had rarely gone a single Sunday without at least a dozen people greeting me or asking for advice. Then, as soon as the news got out, not a single person spoke to me. Many of them even turned away when I looked at them. I was deeply grieved that they seemed to judge me without even knowing what happened or how hard we tried to make things work. As I sat in that service, I realized why some people in similar situations leave their church. A few even abandon the faith completely because of the guilt and rejection they feel in the one place they should never feel it. I expected a bit of judgment, but I also expected at least a few people to reach out to me in love, offer to pray for me or even encourage me. Yet, only one couple in the entire congregation reached out to me and made a point to sit with me often.

Though many people outwardly abandoned me, God never left me or failed me. He walked through the whole ordeal beside me and reminded me to act with integrity in spite of how others were treating me. Thankfully, He also provided support through my business partners who encouraged me, prayed for me and stood by me faithfully. For the first time, I realized how much they loved me unconditionally and their friendship was a huge blessing to me. Nothing reveals your true friends like a serious life crisis.

I truly wanted to deal with my dilemma in the healthiest way possible, but I felt completely ignorant of what that would involve. Counseling was a big help, yet, I longed to understand more deeply how divorce would affect my life and the lives of my loved ones in the future. I hoped that by studying up on the subject I could avoid more poor choices. To cope with my situation, I continued to read several books about divorce and divorce recovery. Learning as much as I could through reading and research seemed like my best chance for rehabilitation and reconciliation.

>> **Nothing reveals your true friends like a serious life crisis.**

I was shocked at what I learned. I had forgotten much of what was happening in my world during my dating years. As I studied the divorce statistics for the previous 70 years, I saw my past in a whole new light. I was married in the 60's when a huge change was taking place in America. My generation seemingly decided that the rules about sex outside of marriage were old fashioned and unnecessary. The Sexual Revolution was under way and relational boundaries were being redefined.

When I was a young child, I remember watching wholesome movies and television shows focused on family values. On screen couples slept in separate beds, foul language was minimal and many shows had valuable life lessons to impart on younger generations. There was the occasional kiss and romantic innuendo, but there were set boundaries on what was audience appropriate. By the time I was a teenager, the social norms were changing fast. The free love movement was in full swing, drug use had risen significantly and sex was becoming a recreational activity rather than a sacred part of the marriage commitment. Sex before and outside of marriage became the new normal. The once negative stigma on promiscuous men and women nearly evaporated. It was no surprise to me that our new freedom brought with it a number of consequences. Among them was a huge increase in teenage pregnancies, an epidemic of sexually transmitted diseases, a skyrocketing divorce rate, and millions of emotionally wounded people.

As I pondered why the Sexual Revolution had caused such an increase in divorce, I remembered a valuable lesson I learned when I first separated from my wife. Because we often struggled to connect, I had read about what a healthy connection should look like. I learned that there are four different levels in which people can connect: mentally, emotionally, spiritually and physically. When my wife and I were dating, I didn't know what levels of connection were possible. As a result, I neglected to get to know her well enough in each area before we made the decision to spend the rest of our lives together. Because I failed to explore all areas of connection with her, not long after we were married I realized that we honestly knew very little about each other.

As I read more about divorce in America, I realized I was not alone in my struggles. Many other couples within my generation had also decided to marry based on their physical attraction and compatibility, confusing that with real love. While exploring the physical connection seems more exciting, and it will hold a relationship together for as little as a few days or years, reality eventually sets in when connection in the other areas becomes progressively more difficult. When my wife and I noticed our lack of connection in other areas, we both struggled to find common ground to stand on. Compromise was nearly impossible.

Before the drastic relational changes of the 60's, divorce was considered to be unacceptable. For my grandparents and the generations before them, divorce was considered shameful and irresponsible. After the Sexual Revolution, divorce became a frequent and acceptable option for the many couples that had discovered they didn't mesh well at all apart from their physical relationship. After they married, they learned that it was much more difficult to connect on the other three levels and divorce seemed to be the only way out.

It broke my heart to learn that divorce has become a major detour in the lives of about 50 percent of the American population. I was a prime example of how the Sexual Revolution shifted the primary focus of relationships among my generation. I was ashamed that I had blindly followed along with the crowd and now I was paying for my ignorance and poor choices. It made me sick and sad inside. The last thing I wanted was to become overwhelmed with my need for companionship and settle for a selfish and shallow relationship that might lead to another divorce. Understanding how I had previously operated made me more determined to concentrate on the mental, emotional and spiritual connection with any potential future relationship. If I neglected to set some healthy boundaries for myself as a newly single man, I would end up repeating my past mistakes and letting my feelings get the best of me.

I began to pray that God would teach me how to keep healthy priorities and boundaries in my life and relationships, as well as maintain my commitment to become a healthier, well-rounded individual. In the past I had let my emotions dictate how I reacted to certain situations. Regretfully, I had been disrespectful to my wife and family on more than one occasion. I never wanted to become that man again and I was willing to do whatever it took to better myself in the future. I decided that I definitely would not go looking for romance, but I wanted to give God room to work in that area if that was His plan.

It felt strange finally taking my wedding ring off. The divorce process was slow and painful, but a huge sense of relief washed over me when it was over. I became anxious to move on to the next chapter of my life. I prayed continually that if God had someone else for me, He would bring her into my life and make it clear that she was the right woman for me. In the meantime, I knew it was essential that I continue to guard my heart and grow as an individual. I was unaware of how valuable the lessons I learned during that time would become.

1: How could getting to know each other in the mental, emotional and spiritual realms before marriage reduce the likelihood of divorce?

_____

_____

_____

_____

2: List one healthy factor and one dysfunctional factor in the home you were brought up in. How did each one affect you?

_____

_____

_____

_____

3: How has divorce affected you or your family?

_____

_____

_____

_____

4: If you have been divorced, what did you do to recover and find healing?

_____

_____

_____

_____

5: If you are married and have areas of disconnect with your spouse, what can you do to develop a deeper and more connected marital bond?

_____

_____

_____

_____

6: In what area do you find it most challenging to connect with your spouse or significant other? What could you do to strengthen the weakest connection?

_____

_____

_____

_____

03 >>

gift OF GRACE

"We come to love not by finding a perfect person, but by learning to see an imperfect person perfectly."

- Sam Keen, *To Love and Be Loved*

As I experienced the painful realities of divorce, I realized how insensitive I had been when counseling couples in the midst of separation or divorce. It made me sad to think that I had likely wounded many friends and acquaintances with my apathetic attitude. The rejection I experienced from people I had known and loved caused me to empathize with the fears and uncertainties of others affected by divorce. I made up my mind to be especially considerate in the future when counseling separated or divorced individuals.

That commitment was tested when I met Roxanne. She walked into my office at Clement Financial Services on a hot summer day in August, 2003. She had called on the advice of church friends and the receptionist randomly placed her on my appointment calendar. Randi, a special-needs woman in her 20's who was in Roxanne's care five days a week, accompanied her. Roxanne introduced herself and Randi, gave Randi a coloring book with crayons and sat down at my conference table. She gently asked her to color and be quiet because we had some important business to discuss. She spoke softly and sincerely, yet, with a firmness that proved to be very effective.

Roxanne then explained that she was recently divorced and would soon be receiving 50 percent of her ex-husband's retirement. They had some debt that she was concerned about trying to pay off. I gathered some information, gave Roxanne a questionnaire to fill out and scheduled her to come back a few days later. I prayed for her and Randi and they slowly headed out the door. I remember wondering how Roxanne could manage Randi since she was taller and heavier than Roxanne, however, she handled her with great ease. I thought to myself, *She must have a lot of patience.* Her obvious love for others was endearing and I respected her kind and sincere attitude toward Randi.

Roxanne returned a week later. We worked on her cash flow and discussed how to handle the retirement funds so she could pay off her and her husband's debts. I reviewed her answers from the questionnaire that I had given her at our first meeting.

She listed the following three goals as her priorities:

1. Pay off all my debt.
2. Take my kids on a nice vacation before my oldest son graduates high school.
3. Find a decent and affordable place for my family to live.

Her answers touched me and her broken spirit stirred me. I was very impressed with her level of commitment to her children's future and it was obvious to me that she loved them deeply. Even with her seemingly grim circumstances, she had an up beat attitude that defied explanation. She listened eagerly and stayed positive throughout the entire meeting. I could tell she was a very determined woman and divorce was not going to bring her down. I was inspired by her tenacity and willingness to do whatever it took to make her life better.

I encouraged her to go through one of the divorce recovery courses being offered by several area churches. I was certain that a recovery course would help her heal and give her confidence. I didn't tell her that I was also searching for a class to attend. She thanked me and told me she would seriously consider it.

I also gave Roxanne several assignments. One was to ask her father if she and her children could live rent-free for a few months in his rental property until she could get on her feet financially. She was nervous about asking her father until I was able to show her how that could really help make her budget work.

Roxanne arrived for her third appointment visibly distraught. She explained that   she had a very uncomfortable discussion with her ex-husband just prior to the meeting. She was concerned that she wouldn't be able to get the child support she needed to adequately provide for her children. She did, however, have some good news. Her father had agreed to let her and the kids move into his rental unit until it was sold. He explained, however, that she would only have 60 days to move out if he received a contract on the property.

As we wrapped up the meeting, I presented her with a schedule of the area divorce recovery courses and urged her once more to attend one. I still didn't tell her why I knew so much about the local divorce recovery schedule. Clement Financial has always been an openly Christian company. It was my custom to pray for every person that I met with before they left. As I prayed for her at the end of the meeting, I asked that God would guide her to a recovery group that would help her through the difficult circumstances.

I finally chose to attend the Saturday evening divorce recovery program at Fellowship Bible Church starting in September, 2003. I had no idea that Roxanne had also chosen that same class. I was shocked when I saw her walk in. When she saw me, she thought I must be the teacher. We laughed and I told her that my own divorce was the reason I knew so much about the classes. She seemed relieved to have someone she knew in class with her. We both faithfully attended each week and usually talked for a few minutes after class. Because I did not feel any attraction toward Roxanne, I felt comfortable being her friend.

One night after class, Roxanne seemed extremely upset, so I asked if she wanted to go get coffee afterward. She replied, "I would love to." I could tell she was stressed, so I tried to encourage her. We spent hours talking and it was obvious that having someone listen to her lifted her spirits.

By the end of the evening, I could tell she felt better after sharing her fears and concerns about the divorce process. I shared some of my experiences with her in hopes that she would find strength in knowing she wasn't the only one struggling with such a huge life change. We had a great time and I left with confidence that her strength had been renewed. I was glad to have found a friend, though I hoped she wouldn't mistake my friendliness for romantic intention. I was still in the healing process and romance was the last thing on my mind.

After the final divorce recovery class, everyone went to Village Inn for coffee. As the group made small talk,

Roxanne described a rather frightening experience she had had the night before. She was leaving a singles gathering at church when she noticed a man in a pickup truck who seemed to be following her. After making several turns trying to lose him, she finally turned into the parking lot of the movie theater where she was supposed to pick up her children. He not only followed her into the parking lot, but also proceeded to pull up behind her and block her car into a parking spot. He then got out of his truck, walked up to her window and talked for the next 45 minutes until her children came out of their movie.

She said she tried to be kind and polite, but his strange behavior absolutely scared her to death. I could see it in her eyes as she told me how he had made her feel trapped and emotionally pressured. As I listened to her story, I was appalled that another professed Christian from her church would blatantly stalk and force his emotional insecurities on a woman he didn't know. No woman should have to put up with that kind of treatment, I thought to myself.

As our group dispersed, I felt I needed to do something constructive with my anger, so I approached Roxanne as we left the restaurant and confessed, "I'm so mad about what that guy did to you. No woman should have to put up with that. There is safety in numbers, so why don't you and I just be buddies? If you need a trustworthy friend to do something with, call me. If I need a friend to do something with, I'll call you."

"I would really like that," she said with a trusting smile. We exchanged cell phone numbers. I felt a sense of peace sweep over me as she turned and walked to her car. I was satisfied that I had made her feel supported and maybe a little less afraid.

The next day was Sunday. To prove that I was serious about being friends, I called Roxanne and asked if she would like to go with me to Bella Vista and walk the trail around the lake as I did every Sunday. I hoped that by being the first to invite her out she would feel more comfortable calling me when she needed someone. Starting around the 1.8 mile trail, I pointed at a crack in the sidewalk and told her that I would share my life story with her until we came back around to that crack, Then she could tell me her story on the second trip around.

Time passed quickly as we walked and talked. Soon we made two loops around the trail. The conversation continued for another couple of hours as we sat on a bench by the lake. She told me about her childhood on a small farm where she was raised and shared stories about church camp and growing up in a small holiness church.

She recounted the struggles she faced in her previous marriage, but when she talked about her kids I could see a sparkle in her eyes. It was obvious that she treasured them most.

As I told Roxanne my life story, we noticed that our lives had striking similarities. We both got married at a young age and encountered difficulties in our marriages shortly after we tied the knot. At several points in our lives we had lived in the same town and never managed to meet. She had attended the same school as my daughter, Lynn, and her sister had worked for me several years before. As we said our goodbyes, I gave her a friendly hug. She mentioned that she had passes to the Silver Dollar City amusement park in Branson, Missouri. It was only a two hour drive from Bentonville, and she invited me to go with her to view the Christmas lights the following Sunday. I postponed giving her an answer because although I wanted to be her buddy, I didn't want to lead her on or do anything that appeared too much like a date.

Since separating from my wife 16 months before, I had hardly talked to another woman unless she was a client or a relative. The last thing I needed was for anyone to say that I must have left my wife for another woman. Furthermore, the thought of getting into another relationship that could possibly end in divorce was a very scary one. I had read about how divorced people are often attracted to the same things in another person that attracted them to their first spouse. They remarry, have the same problems and end up divorced again shortly thereafter.

The easy part for me was that I didn't have any romantic attraction toward Roxanne at that time. I thought surely that meant she was a "safe" friend.

When I missed a call from her a few days later, I felt a twinge of sadness. I realized that I liked having a friend and I wished I had been able to talk to her. It dawned on me how much I enjoyed our walk together and having someone around with whom I could easily relate. While Roxanne was out of town for the holidays I missed her friendship more than I thought I would. I decided that if she still wanted to go to Silver Dollar City when she got back, I would go. When she arrived home after the Christmas holiday, she called to tell me about her trip. We discussed going to Silver Dollar City again and agreed to leave right after church the following Sunday.

When she tapped on my door Sunday morning, I remember opening it and realizing how pretty she looked. She was wearing a stylish white sweater with a bright red scarf, which accented her cherry red lipstick and nail polish. That was the first time I really noticed her as a woman rather than just a friend. Her beautiful green eyes seemed to shine in the sunlight and her soft smile made my heart melt. I was shocked that I hadn't noticed how lovely she was before then. I suddenly realized that my seemingly "safe" friend was actually a very pretty lady.

On our 90-minute drive, she expressed her frustrations about Christmas and how her relationships had changed with her former in-laws and friends since the divorce. I related how the people at my church who had once eagerly sought my advice as a speaker and a financial counselor avoided me like the plague after my separation from my wife. Just before arriving at Silver Dollar City, we agreed to stop talking about divorce and ex-spouses and just enjoy the Christmas lights.

Over a light lunch, I began to tell her about a book I read by Gary Chapman called *The Five Love Languages.* I found it a compelling read which gave me some amazing insights into how to better relate to others as well as how to understand myself. The author defines the five love languages as: touch, words of affirmation, acts of service, quality time and giving and receiving gifts. He also included a simple test to identify one's individual love language. I gave the test to Roxanne and discovered that we shared the same primary love language—touch. I was intrigued at finding yet another thing we had in common. For the first time, I felt a spark of romance between us. As we looked into each other's eyes, I sensed that we both wondered if the purpose of our meeting was for more than just a friendship.

After lunch we decided to attend the Dickens Christmas Carol show. We were thrilled to find two seats in row three of a nearly full auditorium. As the show started, I felt like a kid again, going to the movies with a girl for the first time. I really wanted to reach over and hold Roxanne's hand, but my nerves were getting the best of me. There I was, a 53-year-old man who had once been married for more than 30 years, completely terrified to reach over and take her hand.

I tried to work up the courage to make my move, when Roxanne cautiously slipped her arm in under mine, which made it easy for me to slide my hand down and hold hers. After more than a year of heartache, isolation and a profound sense of rejection, that connection with another person was indescribable.

For the next few hours, nothing else seemed to matter. Those clasped hands brought a sense of peace, joy, and well-being that I had not experienced in a long time. At the end of the day when we started to head home, I decided I would give her a kiss. As I tried to plan out how I would make my move, a wave of anxiety swept over me. I suddenly felt like a 12-year-old boy, awkward and unsure of myself. As we neared the park exit, I spotted a romantic nook nearby with Christmas lights hanging overhead and thought that when we reached it, I would swoop in for a smooch. Unfortunately, when we arrived, my nerves got the best of me and I chickened out. I was mad at myself all the way to the truck, disappointed that I had missed my opportunity. Thankfully, Roxanne didn't seem to notice my failed romantic gesture and when we got to the truck she looked into my eyes and said, "Thank you for such an amazing day." Then, she leaned forward as if she was just waiting for me to make my move. The kiss that followed came naturally. At that moment, I felt like a man who had been lost in a desert for years and had finally been given a fresh drink of cool water. My life, which had previously felt scattered and out of control, suddenly felt right.

>**We soon realized that we were not two teens holding hands, but two needy adults that had been deprived of intimacy, both emotionally and physically for a long time.**

The conversation on the way home moved to our hopes and dreams. We soon realized that we were not two teens holding hands, but two needy adults that had been deprived of intimacy, both emotionally and physically for a long time. We had more in common than I ever thought we could. Both of us had struggled through many challenges of newly single life after divorce and had felt rejected and isolated for a long time. We were equally afraid to test out a new relationship because we felt that we had both failed in our previous marriages. We were both concerned and dedicated parents and agreed, that because of our past mistakes, we would need to be very careful how we handled our relationship with each other. It was surprisingly easy to share things with each other that we never thought we would feel comfortable talking about. We each shared a sense of safety in the honesty between us.

The following evening we were able to get together to discuss the events of the previous day a bit more rationally. We knew that if we wanted to do things radically different than we had in our first marriages, we needed to start off on the right foot and keep going forward until God revealed His full plan for us. Since touch was our primary love language, we knew the desire to get to know each other in a meaningful way could likely be derailed if sex was introduced into the equation. When romance is first felt between two needy people who have so much in common, it is easy for those feelings to get overwhelming and create attachments that could be unhealthy if marriage is not God's plan. Knowing that our physical attraction was already strong, we agreed that our most important goal should be to get to know each other in a deep and intimate way in the other areas of connection in order to determine if we were compatible for marriage. We agreed that we had to be proactive if we honestly wanted to learn as much about each other as possible. With that in mind, we realized that we needed to set boundaries that would create a safe place for us to share and grow together. We honestly tried to assess all the risks that could be involved, and as a result, we made the following guidelines that would create safe boundaries for us:

1. No sexual kissing.
2. No sexual touching.
3. If one of us felt aroused, we would commit to stop, move away and start a different activity.

We prayed together and told God we were serious about these commitments and asked Him for the strength to stick to them. We channeled all our energy into getting to know each other and committed to pray for each other daily. We spent every evening we could together reading and discussing books, writing questions for each other and sharing our answers, or just walking and talking.

We would often write questions for each other such as: How do you feel about this subject? What do you like? What do you want out of a romantic relationship? What would the perfect life look like? What kind of church would you like to attend? As we thoughtfully wrote down our own answers to all the questions and shared them with each other, we found that we were very well matched. The most significant discovery that we made was that we were able to bond spiritually with very little effort. I could count on her to be my accountability partner, and we shared a unique peace each time we prayed together.

One of the resources we used to get to know each other better in the four areas of connection was a book called *Fall in Love Stay in Love* by Willard F. Harley, Jr. It presented different relationship issues for us to discuss. From that book, we developed three commitments that built a foundation of complete honesty:

1. If you think it - say it.
2. If you feel it - share it.
3. If you wonder about it - ask.

By being open and transparent with each other, we became increasingly more emotionally intimate. Our radical honesty took us places neither of us had ever been. We trusted each other with our deepest secrets, hurts, failures, hopes, ambitions and dreams. It was amazing to see how that level of trust led us to being real with each other. So, when we noticed how completely different we were from one another in our thought processes, we listened to the other viewpoint with an open heart and began to see and experience life in a whole new way, drawing us closer together. We cemented our mental and emotional bond by refusing to allow anything unsaid to cause a rift between us. God took two completely different personality types and melded them together to create two stronger individuals and one amazingly well rounded unit. Each new discovery bonded us more. Without a doubt there were some profoundly difficult things to share, but we were determined to be as vulnerable as possible. Our love grew exponentially as we revealed our deep and difficult secrets.

Soon our hearts were melting together. It was a kind of intimacy that goes light years beyond the intimacy of sexual intercourse. As our mental, emotional, and spiritual connections deepened, our desire for each other and for physical intimacy intensified. We often found ourselves taking a break and doing something different in order to fulfill our commitment to purity. We would often take a walk or play the *What Would Jesus Do?* board game. That one definitely helped change the mood, in addition to giving us insight into what each of us would do when a morally questionable situation came up. When that didn't help or it felt impossible to calm ourselves, one of us would start praying out loud.

One evening one of our get to know you questions was, "Where have you always wanted to go?" Roxanne's answer was, "Niagara Falls. I love waterfalls." After some playful teasing about that being sort of old-fashioned, I told her that if we ever got married, we could go to Niagara Falls for our honeymoon.

At that time, Roxanne's children were 12, 13 and 16 years old. We agreed that I did not need to meet them until we were positive that our relationship had serious potential. As we realized how much we were falling for each other, Roxanne finally shared the news with the kids. They said they saw a twinkle in her eyes they had never seen before. Thankfully they were supportive of her seeing me even though they hadn't met me yet.

After meeting her three children, we started attending their football and basketball games as a couple. They became part of the "get to know you" process. I quickly grew to love Travis, Bobby and Tiffany and was convinced that we would do well as a family. I knew we would face our fair share of challenges, but I was certain that I could help to provide a huge sense of stability for them that a single mom would have trouble providing on her own. A big part of me felt called to help Roxanne raise them in a healthy and stable environment. Though I was partially fearful that the process would have difficult moments, I sensed that we could be a tremendous blessing to each other's lives.

The more intimately Roxanne and I got to know each other the more confident I was that God had brought her into my life as an amazing gift. I often felt undeserving of His generosity and favor because of my past, but then He would remind me that His love for me is based on grace. It has nothing to do with my past or my failures. When I asked for forgiveness, He responded with grace and mercy. As Roxanne and I took steps in the right direction, He continued to bless our commitment to keep our focus on Him. As our love grew, I was beginning to believe that we were meant to spend the rest of our lives together.

POINTS 2 PONDER
AVOIDING relational disasters ▸ ❯

1: Do you believe physical intimacy early in a relationship can undermine the connection in the mental, emotional and spiritual realms? If so how?

_____

_____

_____

_____

2: What do you feel are the key elements in any relationship that will promote long-term success?

_____

_____

_____

_____

3: How could a commitment to radical honesty change your current relationships?

_____

_____

_____

_____

4: What healthy boundaries would you set early in a potential relationship to help to ensure long-term success?

_____

_____

04 >>

a trail of
MIRACLES

"Faith is taking the first step, even when you don't see the whole staircase."

- Martin Luther King Jr.

When I first began spending time with Roxanne, I was terrified of making a mistake or getting hurt. As time passed, that fear was replaced with peace. I prayed daily for God to guide us in our relationship, something I had neglected to do in my previous marriage. After only four months of dating, I had no doubt that God had given us His blessing and that Roxanne was His special gift to me. What I felt for her was not just a warm fuzzy feeling or a stomach full of butterflies, although those were present—it was a divine calling on my life. I had a deep conviction that God had a unique purpose for us. The only thing left to do was to pop the question.

One Saturday night in early April, 2004, Roxanne and I were cooking dinner in my apartment. I hadn't bought a ring yet, but I simply couldn't wait another moment to ask. After removing our dinner from the stove, I took her in my arms, looked deep into her beautiful green eyes and said, "Roxanne, you make me so happy. I believe God heard our prayers and brought us together. I love you with all my heart and I want to spend the rest of my life with you. Will you marry me?"

A dazzling smile swept across her face and her eyes sparkled as she answered, "Roger, I also believe God brought us together and connected us in a way I have never known. I love you with all my heart and, yes, I will marry you!" We were so happy and so excited that we forgot all about dinner. Tears of joy filled her eyes as we hugged, kissed and danced around the room until we had to reheat our dinner in the microwave.

In case that proposal seemed less than romantic, I decided to compensate for it by making an adventure out of giving her an engagement ring. Her birthday was coming up soon, so I decided to surprise her then. I invited her to my apartment that evening, where I had planned a romantic dinner. When she arrived, I gave her a bouquet of flowers and a card with a poem on it. After dining on my "world class" cooking, I presented her with a small box, which she probably assumed contained a ring. I could tell she was a bit nervous as she opened it, but when she discovered a note instead, she seemed intrigued. The note read, "Let's go on a treasure hunt!" and gave her the first clue.

Giggling as she discovered each new clue, the search finally lead her to a cabinet where I had hidden the ring box with a note above it proposing, "Let's get hitched!" She squealed with delight when she saw it and even did a triple-take. On the third glance, she began to cry. Standing there in that magical moment, she seemed almost afraid to reach out and touch it and continued to stare at it as if she still wasn't sure it was for real. Finally, I said, "Babe, you can take it out of the cabinet if you want." With that, I pulled it out and placed it on her finger. She wrapped her arms around me and simply said, "I love you." For the next few hours, we talked about wedding details, made plans for future trips and adventures we would have together and decided to write our own vows. It was a night I will never forget.

I could hardly wait to begin our new life together. Unfortunately, our children weren't as enthusiastic about the news. My two daughters, though adults with children of their own, were the most upset. I knew they wouldn't be happy about it, but I underestimated how much. I hadn't been around nearly enough as a dad, thanks to my habit of overworking, so the thought of having to compete for time with three more children was not a welcome one for them. I tried to reassure them, and reminded them that I'd always be their dad. Still, I suspected that it would take them some time to get comfortable with the idea.

Roxanne's oldest, Travis, was equally disgruntled. I understood his skepticism because he didn't get much of a chance to get to know me before the engagement. Bobby and Tiffany were both glad that their mom had found someone to make her happy. Although they didn't know me well either, they liked me. They were also excited about the idea of moving out of their rental home. Roxanne and I hoped and prayed that in time they would all grow closer together and enjoy being a family. We didn't want to rush anyone into it and agreed to let God do the work of uniting us in His time.

A few days later, a series of events occurred that we

recognized as God's orchestration of our lives. The details came together in a way that could have only been His hand at work. He answered prayers with record speed and blessed us with some of the best times of our lives.

Because Roxanne and I wanted to marry as soon as it was reasonably possible, we began planning immediately. I had promised her a honeymoon in Niagara Falls. We had also discussed taking all our kids and grandkids somewhere together so they could really bond. Unexpectedly, Roxanne's father sold the rental house where she and the kids had been living and informed her that she had to be out of the house by the end of May, 60 days later. At the same time, I learned that, through my business I had been awarded an all-expense-paid trip for my spouse and me to go to Orlando, Florida, the second week of June. Finally, Roxanne's son, Travis, won a trip to Orlando with a humanitarian organization that was scheduled a few days after my trip to Orlando.

With all those factors in mind, Roxanne and I concluded that we needed to plan a wedding for May 27—only six weeks later. We would go on a honeymoon to Niagara Falls, come home, repack and take all our kid and grandkids to Orlando for a week. Meanwhile, we knew we had to purchase a home and move in before the wedding. We bowed our heads and prayed, *God, this looks pretty impossible to pull off. We are basically asking You for a series of miracles. Lord, the way this has all happened, it appears that You are in it. Now we are trusting You to bring all the details together.*

The next evening, Roxanne and I reviewed our list of prerequisites for a house. With three active teenagers all involved in sports, we needed a home that fit our requirements for space and layout. We also wanted it to be located in the kids' current school district so they would not have to start over making friends somewhere new. We needed to be able to move into the new house within 45 days in order for Roxanne and the kids to be out of the rental house in time. As if that wasn't difficult enough, there were also budget considerations.

I had made a commitment several years prior not to go into debt for anything, including a home. I had given up most of my assets, except for my business, in my divorce. After carefully calculating what we could spend on a house, I shared that number with Roxanne. I saw her tear up as she said "Sweetheart, I don't see how we can find the house we just described for that amount." I replied, "Babe, we probably can't, but God can. Let's ask Him right now to do just that."

>> **I made a commitment several years prior not to go into debt for anything, including a home.**

Then the adventure began. After praying, we drove around several subdivisions looking for "For Sale" signs. We found a potential house that was obviously unoccupied with a real estate sign in the yard. We called the realtor and she agreed to meet us there right away. We liked the home, but it needed so much work that the cost would be above our means. When the realtor asked what we were looking for, we described our situation and she promised to continue looking. We viewed three or four more houses over the next few days, but none of them fit our needs. Then the miracles began to happen.

One week after we first met the realtor, she called and said, "Roger, I think I found your house. It went on the market last night. It meets all your criteria. You need to look at it now. I don't think it will last through the weekend."

We hurried to meet her at the address. The house was perfect. The price was exactly what we needed and it was in unbelievable condition. We immediately went to her office to fill out a contract. She called the listing realtor to tell her an offer would be coming and learned that they already had an offer in hand which the homeowners were on their way to review. Our realtor replied, "You will have a second offer there in 20 minutes." Knowing that the other bid was waiting for them, we submitted a full-price bid. Within an hour, they accepted our offer. If we had hesitated even 30 minutes or our realtor hadn't called ahead, the house would have been sold. God miraculously provided a house for a price we could afford and it was available for Roxanne and the kids to move into exactly when we needed it. We had a contract on the house, but everything had to work out perfectly for us to be able to move in on schedule. We had less than four weeks to close on the house, have the sellers move out, pack up both our households and get Roxanne and the kids moved in. In other words, we needed another miracle. After buying and selling several homes, I knew that the closing process would have to go off without a hitch in order for us to meet our deadline. I knew we would be cutting it close to get everything done in time, so Roxanne and I prayed for a flawless closing. It turned out to be the most trouble-free closing I ever had and the only closing in which the home inspector cited, "No repairs needed." I could hardly believe how easy it was.

Our honeymoon and trip to Florida would require us both to be off work for two weeks, so neither of us could afford to take off for the move. It was imperative that the sellers vacate the home by the weekend before the wedding. We walked into the house on the Friday evening before the wedding and discovered that, not only were they moved out, but they had also left the house spotlessly clean and perfectly ready for us to occupy. Roxanne was out of her dad's house on time and she and the kids were completely moved in by the Sunday evening before our wedding.

Having a trip with all our kids and grandkids so they could bond was very important to us. The trips that Travis and I had won provided free airfare for three people; however, that left ten people I would need to provide with airfare within 30 days. We also had to find a place to stay that we could afford at a very busy time in Orlando. Early one morning before work, I sat down at my computer in an attempt to find seats and lodging as inexpensively as possible. First, I prayed, "Lord, You opened the door for this Orlando thing. Now we need You to provide for the rest of our family. We need some cheap flights and a reasonable place to stay." I was concerned that since we only had 30 days to plan, the flights would be expensive and possibly beyond our means. It was then that God amazed us with the biggest miracle of our story yet. Within two hours, I was able to find everyone a free ticket using the air miles I had collected during the past five years. I was also able to rent a home large enough for all our kids and grandkids that also had a huge kitchen and even a swimming pool.

Roxanne's best friend, Tina, offered to have the wedding in her backyard. She also volunteered to help plan it, promising that it would be beautiful. She took care of every detail and even created an exquisite white arch under which we would exchange our vows. My administrative assistant, Laurie, volunteered to be the wedding planner and coordinated the event like a professional. On Thursday evening during the rehearsal, the sky was black and threatening. Roxanne and I said a little prayer asking God to hold back the storm until the rehearsal was over. Fortunately, we all made it home safe and dry just before the rain began.

When our special day arrived, I started getting a little nervous thinking about how drastically my life was about to change. I would soon be responsible for four individuals whom I loved dearly. As I put on my tuxedo, I prayed that God would enable me to be the best husband and example for Roxanne's children that I could be. Confident that God had heard my prayer, I marched out to mingle with the guests. I was visiting with the groomsmen on the porch when I suddenly became aware of a draft on my bottom half.

When I looked down, to my horror, my trousers were around my ankles. Roxanne and I had been on a diet throughout our engagement and I had apparently lost more weight than I realized. Roxanne's son, Bobby, ran into the house frantically searching for some safety pins as I pulled up my trousers, holding on to them for dear life. As he pinned my pants I attempted to regain my composure. Thankfully, he got them fixed up pretty quickly and to my great relief, only a few guests were flashed.

To add to the hilarity of the day, Tina's pet goat, Dolly, was making a scene. She usually roamed their yard freely, but for the big day she had to be tied up in the far corner of the yard

Tina's pet goat, Dolly

so she wouldn't disturb the wedding festivities. She was not at all happy to be in captivity, and retaliated with constant bleating. I hoped that she would have exhausted herself by the time the wedding started, but that was not the case.

I tried to tune Dolly out by recollecting the events of the previous year. It had been the most challenging and frightening year of my life. Out of the ashes of my broken dreams and relationships, God brought healing, hope, and ultimately, Roxanne. He had given me a blessing of grace far beyond anything I could have asked for. Standing before our guests and waiting for Roxanne, my heart could barely contain the joy inside.

As I continued my musing, I realized that at any moment Roxanne would come walking through that door and pledge her love to me for the rest of her life. Though a bit concerned that I might break into laughter if the loud and persistent goat serenaded our exchange of vows, I was overwhelmed with gratitude. I was especially elated that Roxanne had missed the pre-wedding peep show. A little worried that the safety pins holding up my trousers might give way in the middle of the service, I tried hard to refrain from any sudden movements.

All of our children and grandchildren were present and the yard was filled with our cherished friends and family. Even Randi was present. She was given the special task of having everyone sign the guest book as they arrived.

*Roxanne and her
friend, Randi*

The huge smile on her face told me she couldn't have been more proud that Roxanne had included her in her special day. Roxanne even bought her a dress that matched all the other bridesmaids. Had I been a guest at the wedding I might have guessed that she was the bride. She could hardly contain her excitement as she greeted each person as they signed in.

One by one, the wedding party made their way up to the arch where I stood waiting. Soft music played in the background and the birds were singing as Roxanne stepped out in her flowing white dress. For a moment, I felt as if I'd drifted into a fantasy. Like an angel, she floated toward me smiling from ear to ear, aglow with the same warmth and serenity that I had grown to love about her. Her soft blonde curls were pinned up with lovely white flowers. Pearl jewelry completed her elegant look. Her beautiful green eyes radiated with expectation. She was breathtaking— and I was convinced that I was the luckiest man in the world.

*Lynn, Casey, me,
Roxanne, Tiffany,
Travis and Bobby*

Once Roxanne was standing at my side, I reached out and took her hand in mine. Laurie's husband, Paul, performed the ceremony. He opened the service by talking about building memories and keeping God first in our lives and marriage. I smiled as I remembered how we had danced in my kitchen as we envisioned our wedding day and how we had committed every moment to God, every step of the way.

We had arranged for a song that we each dedicated to the other to be played before we recited our vows. The song I chose for her was "She's More" by Andy Griggs. I sang along to her softly as she smiled up at me, blinking back tears. The song she chose for me was "When You Say You Love Me" by Josh Groban. Looking into each other's eyes, every fear and doubt either of us may have had about the future melted away. Since Roxanne and I found traditional wedding vows to be lacking the sentiment and passion that we felt for each other, we chose to write our own.

Our Wedding Vows

I promise always to strive, not only to love you, but to be lovable. Not only to honor you, but to be honorable. Not only to cherish you, but to be one that can be cherished. Not only to trust you, but to be trustworthy. I promise always to strive to keep Jesus Christ as the Lord of my life and to look to Him for strength, guidance, wisdom and help. I promise always to strive to love you and stand by you in sickness or health, in abundance or need, in whatever circumstances we might find ourselves. I promise always to strive to meet your needs, to protect our relationship in such a way that your love bank stays full and running over so that you will never have need for another. I promise to love your children as my children. I will cherish you always, love you unconditionally and be with you through good times and bad. You are not only my lover, you are my best friend.

After our vows, my niece, Nicole, sang, "When You Believe" by Mariah Carey and Whitney Houston. Listening to the words, I realized that Roxanne was truly the greatest miracle of my life.

Finally, we sealed the deal with a kiss. I was so happy that I danced a little jig as I walked her off the platform. We ate cake, took pictures and visited with old friends. As Roxanne thanked the guests for coming, my daughter, Lynn, hijacked the video camera. She decided to tell our love story to the tune of the Brady Bunch theme song as the goat continued to bleat in the background. Those who were there will likely never forget the sound effects of our wedding celebration.

Roxanne overlooking Niagra Falls

I kept my promise to Roxanne to go to Niagara Falls for our honeymoon. I managed to secure an incredible room overlooking the falls. When Roxanne got her first look out over the falls, tears streamed down her face as she said, "This is the most beautiful thing I've ever seen!" Thrilled to be giving her the honeymoon of her dreams, all I could say was, "Thank you, Lord." Because of the level of intimacy we had experienced mentally and emotionally in the process of getting to know each other, the physical intimacy we shared during our honeymoon surpassed our greatest expectations and bonded us together spiritually. We experienced the true meaning of the biblical reference for "the two will become one."

The next day we savored the falls from every angle, marveling at God's handiwork and praising Him for the amazing gift He had given us in each other. After a long day of exploring, we relaxed in our Jacuzzi tub. We dreamed aloud about our future together, trips we wanted to take, and sights we wanted to see.

We arrived home a couple of days before it was time to head out for our trip to Florida with the rest of the family. We ended up being separated into three different flights, going to three different connecting cities, yet, we all arrived in Orlando within 90 minutes of each other. The timing of our flights could not have been more perfect. Since I arrived first, I was able to have two vans ready and waiting for everyone. Roxanne and I checked into our hotel inside the Disney complex while the kids went to the vacation home I had rented only five miles across town. Later that evening we enjoyed dinner together and prepared for our trip to Disney World the following day. Roxanne and I took the youngest grandkids to Fantasy Land while Travis, Bobby and Tiffany went to ride roller coasters with my daughter, Casey, and my grandson, Jon. The kids teased me about the huge backpacks I hauled around with all our food in them, but we saved hundreds of dollars on food and drinks while enjoying the four Disney parks. In the evenings, all the kids gathered at the house to swim in the pool while Roxanne and I relished quality alone time.

We were so thankful that we were able to take 13 people to Orlando for an entire week for a crazy affordable price. Everyone had a blast. Just as we had hoped, the kids and grandkids were like best buddies by the time we arrived back home. That trip sealed the deal for all of us and we've remained close ever since. We prayed for some ridiculous things and each time God answered without hesitation. He proved to us that He wants to be involved in our lives at every level. Be it big or small, good or bad, extraordinary or routine, exciting or mundane, He longs to be there with us through it all. He is still doing miracles in the world today. He demonstrated that to us without question.

POINTS2PONDER
A present GOD ▸ ›

1: Describe a miracle God has done in your life or in the life of someone you know.

_____

_____

_____

_____

2: How have you seen God work, even in the small things, in your everyday life?

_____

_____

_____

_____

3: Share something in your life that you are struggling to believe that God can handle:

_____

_____

_____

_____

4: Describe a defining moment in your past when you knew God could be trusted and believed He could accomplish anything in your life, big or small:

_____

_____

family is not about

BLOOD...

it's about

LOVE

"Love doesn't just happen to you. Love is a choice and it represents a commitment."

- Rick Warren

I'd love to tell you that after our fairytale beginning we lived happily ever after, because, at this point, it may seem that God was like a generous grandfather in the sky miraculously answering prayers and making all our dreams come true. Unfortunately, no family is perfect, and we were no exception. After our incredible honeymoon, life seemed to settle into a more ordinary routine.

We had the normal struggles you would expect, not only from a blended family, but also from a family with three teenagers. We endured the typical hassles with ex-spouses, the dynamic of a new man in the house for Roxanne's kids and a new grandma hanging around with Pop, which is what the grandkids call me. It was tense at times and occasionally it seemed a bit like a nightmare. Yet, we knew our children and grandchildren all heard us make a promise on our wedding day to love each other's children as if they were our own. Roxanne and I were totally committed to making that happen.

Let's pretend for a moment that this is a play and I'll share a little about all the characters. First, are my two daughters from my previous marriage, who were no longer living at home. Lynn, at 32, is happily married with one son, Jon. She's an independent and determined woman with a passion for reaching troubled and needy children. Casey, at 26, is a very giving mother and loving pastor's wife who is as dedicated to her ministry as she is to her family.

Roxanne has three children. Travis, only 16 at the time, is a fun loving, hardworking young man who had assumed many of the responsibilities as the man of the house after his parents' divorce. Bobby, at 14, is a running back at Oakdale Junior High who lived and breathed football. Animated and energetic, Roxanne's only daughter, Tiffany is 12. She was already the life of the party wherever she went. Though hilarious and unpredictable, she had been on two mission trips outside the U.S and is very committed to her church youth group.

I also have four grandchildren. Lynn's son, at that time,

Jon, is 15 and the oldest of all my grandchildren. Like his mother, he is very tenderhearted. He also loves soccer and especially loves his Pop. Casey's oldest boy, Jarvis, is four and already showing potential as a future athlete. He loves lizards and jumping into piles of leaves in the fall. Carson, at three, is the middle child and clearly has a superhero complex, as he spends most of his time in a caped costume. Riley, just shy of two, already has a personality primed for becoming the first female president, ready to take charge of any given situation.

Our plethora of personalities created many challenges that Roxanne and I had never faced before. Since I am a planner by nature and knew that we needed a plan to succeed as a family, I suggested that Roxanne and I be proactive about how we ran

Jarvis, Jon, Carson, me and Riley

Carson in his Superman costume

our household by writing a list of the things that were most important to us in family life. We spent hours talking about what we expected and how we would respond if certain situations arose. We even compiled a list of goals and commitments to keep us on track. The fact that neither of us had established healthy home boundaries in our previous relationships made the subject especially important to us. The following are some of the commitments we made to build a healthy family:

1. Pray both individually and together for our children and grandchildren each day.

2. Never disagree in front of them. Always present a united front to them and then discuss the matter in private if we have any concerns or conflicting ideas about the situation.

3. Always speak respectfully and expect respect in return.

4. Attend church as a family every Sunday and encourage the children to be involved with Bible studies and other church-related activities.

5. Eat together as a family whenever possible and never have the TV on during meals.

6. Pray together before each meal.

7. Try our best to attend the games, programs, and activities that are important to our children and grandchildren.

8. Express unconditional love to our children and their friends.

9. Find ways to tell the children we love them on a daily basis.

10. Provide a warm, receptive, accepting place for their friends to enjoy.

11. Plan family activities to maintain a strong family bond.

12. Never criticize or create a sense of competition with an ex-spouse.

13. Model Christ-like behavior, a Christ-like home and a Christ-like marriage.

14. Give everyone time to adjust to the changes while trying to understand each person's perspective.

15. Schedule one-on-one time with each individual in order to get to know one another better.

I usually went to work before the kids were up, so I left them a note on the bar each morning telling them to have a good day and that I loved them. I also included a quote, a Bible verse, or some word of wisdom. It was important to me that they knew I was thinking about them and praying for them every day. I never tried to force them to say they loved me or call me Dad. I knew if I consistently loved them that it would eventually all work out. And it did.

As they grew to know me better and realized how dedicated I was to caring for them and their mother, they all opened up to me and treated me as their father figure. For Father's Day, each of them eventually got me a picture frame reading "World's Greatest Dad," complete with a photo of us together. Roxanne and I believed that an important aspect of loving our kids was choosing to love their friends as well. We knew how important their friends were to them and we wanted our home to be a safe and inviting place for them and their friends. We wanted our kids to be more comfortable at our house than they were anywhere else so that they would want to hang out at home. As a result of our efforts, both our children and their friends loved to spend time at our house. They became an extended part of our family. We always had extra kids around, even in our family Christmas pictures.

Our open door policy gave us a great opportunity to minister to them and set an example for our children of how to have healthy, godly relationships. Roxanne loved, hugged, fed and encouraged every kid our children brought home. She treated them all like special people and many of them continued to be her friend even after our kids moved on.

Each time the kids brought home a new friend, I began trying to determine their love language. That would clue our family in to what made that particular person feel loved. We had seen how learning the love languages of each of our kids and grandkids had enabled us to better relate to them, help them feel loved and show them how to love others more effectively.

Each of the kids living in our home had different love languages. Because Travis needs and desires words of affirmation, telling him what a great job he was doing not only motivated him to do even better, but also made him feel loved. Bobby's love language is acts of service, thus he was always quick to say, "thank you," when we dropped him off at the movies or ironed his shirts. He didn't respond well to words of affirmation. His attitude was, "If you really think I'm special, don't just talk about it—do something for me."

If Roxanne and I went a while without spending quality time with Tiffany, she became irritable. Her mom could take her for coffee and thrift store shopping and she would be like a whole new person. Why? Because she felt loved. A year and a half after Roxanne and I were married, our grandson, Jon, moved in with us. His love language is touch. A couple of big hugs make him feel special. He was used to getting hugs from me, so when Roxanne gave him a hug, it was a special treat for him.

The mistake I had often made in my first marriage and when raising my children was that I assumed that loving others the way I understood and received love helped them feel loved. The reality was I needed to learn to love them in their love language, not mine. That is why I firmly believe *The Five Love Languages* by Gary Chapman should be required reading for every human being. What it taught me had a profound effect on how I handled my relationship with Roxanne and how we communicated with our children. Looking back, I wish I had read it when my girls were growing up. I have since found out that Lynn's love language is touch, and Casey's is acts of service. Though I can't go back and change the past, I try very hard now to make up for that lost time by being more sensitive to their love languages.

After reading *The Five Love Languages,* I gave it to Roxanne to read and told her when she finished I would love to talk more with her about it. When she finished, we realized our primary and secondary love languages were the same— touch and quality time. We spent hours talking about what we learned and how it had affected our lives. Afterwards we promised each other that we'd always try to love each other the way each of us needed to feel most loved and satisfied.

By sharing what we learned with each other, we quickly concluded that love is not simply a feeling—it's a choice. We wanted to make loving choices every day as often as possible. Feelings are fickle and can change according to circumstances. It's an easy move from, "I love you," to "I hate you," when we gauge our relationships on feelings. On the other hand, if we choose to love someone, our love does not diminish in hard times, but is strengthened as we find ways to overcome the obstacles that are certain to arise.

Roxanne and I tried and proved that principle in our home over and over again. The power of loving choices is what kept us close, helped heal the wounds of our pasts and made our family unique. The difference in the way we chose to love each other was obvious to anyone who knew us. It often had a surprisingly meaningful impact on their lives.

Roxanne and I never shied away from appropriate discipline, but we were careful with how we chose to discipline our kids and the attitude we presented it with. In my ministry I had counseled many adults who shared that the words they remembered most from their parents were hateful, critical and mean-spirited words spoken in a moment of anger. Those words would often ring in their minds for the rest of their lives, causing them grief, and spilling over into how they treated their own children. That experience made me think twice about how to communicate with my own kids.

When an issue arose with our children, we would first step back and take a moment to allow our emotions to settle. We actively chose not to react to difficult situations based on our feelings or fears. Instead we prayed about what to do and then made a decision about which one of us would be able to talk with them about it without getting angry or acting impulsively. We then made a plan on how to communicate what needed to be said and agreed on what disciplinary action needed to be taken. In most cases, I would have a heart-to-heart talk with them, tell them what they had done wrong and why. Then I would give them a chance to correct the behavior before moving forward with a more severe punishment, such as being grounded or taking away their phone or driving privileges. Because they knew I was a man of my word, I never had to tell one of them twice. They knew I was serious and made adjustments accordingly.

Roxanne and I believed that if we wanted to have healthy children, we needed to have a healthy marriage. Nothing makes a child feel more secure than knowing his or her parents love one another. When couples argue or disrespect each other in front of their children, the children become anxious, insecure and fearful that their family will fall apart at any moment. We didn't want our kids to be afraid of that possibility. Children often repeat the same behavior in their relationships, perpetuating the cycle of unhealthy relational habits. I had seen that happen in my own life and hoped that by working hard to have a strong bond with my wife and kids, they would never make the same mistakes I had made.

In order for our family to thrive, we knew that we also needed to protect our time together. We made it a priority to schedule a romantic rendezvous as often as possible. During our first year of marriage, Roxanne worked from 6 AM to 2 PM. We had what we called our, "two o'clock." Every Monday, Wednesday and Friday, I left work at two o'clock and met Roxanne at home. We spent an hour together before I returned to work. That was our special time for sharing. When we were home for the evening, we went to our room at 9 PM. We told the kids goodnight and they knew not to bother us except in an emergency. We recognized that if we wanted to have the best relationship possible, we had to proactively work at it.

It was also important that we communicated our love. "I love you," was the first thing we would say to each other in the morning and the last thing we would say before we went to sleep. We said it on the phone, in text messages and on notes frequently left for each other. The only time during our marriage that I did not say, "I love you," in person was when she was on a trip out of the country and electronic communications were not possible. Even so, on those occasions I would write little love notes and hide them in her suitcase so that she would find them during her trip. That was a romantic trick she taught me when I had traveled alone. It made me feel incredibly special to open up my suitcase and find her unexpected notes.

For the first five years of our marriage, we gave each other monthly anniversary cards. I also brought her fresh flowers regularly. Our gifts didn't need to be expensive. A simple bouquet or a homemade card let her know I was committed to expressing my love for her often. She highly valued the thought behind those little gifts. Real love is not about rituals and doesn't come with a price tag. It is often the little things that mean the most.

We promised that we would never go to sleep upset with each other. Our commitment to, "If you think it, say it; if you feel it, share it; if you wonder about it, ask." forced us to deal with things quickly before they grew into bigger problems. There were many nights that I said, "Babe, I feel like something is bothering you or is on your mind." Then I would listen quietly, giving her the freedom to talk about whatever it was. There were times when she found it difficult to express what she was feeling.

She would take several minutes to collect her thoughts before telling me what was on her mind. Because I listened patiently, she grew to understand that her feelings really mattered to me and vice versa. That radical honesty deepened our respect for each other. There was never a night when we went to sleep without peace and unity of heart.

Most mornings we read a daily devotion and prayed together before I went to work. As we prayed for our children and grandchildren, we asked God for the ability to love every member of our family unconditionally and to overcome any possible obstacle that might prevent us from faithfully choosing to love. God honored that request and we watched in awe as we saw that love spill over into the lives of friends and many others that we came in contact with.

I do not want to embarrass our adult children by sharing specific incidents from their lives, but I know each one of them would agree that divorce and remarriage are difficult for everyone involved. Restructuring a family is an emotional, scary and often painful experience. Our blended family made it through those challenging days with patience, understanding, kindness, grace, prayer, perseverance, honest communication, hard work and love. Each loving choice brought us closer and strengthened our trust for one another. As a result, today we have one of the most loving families I've ever known— not because of blood, but because we choose to love.

POINTS 2 PONDER
BUILDING a family of LOVE ▸ ≫

1. Consider each of these quotes and decide whether or not you believe they are true and why:

* *"In a marriage, the little things matter the most."*

_____

_____

* *"Nothing makes children feel more secure than knowing that their parents love each other."*

_____

_____

* *"Love is not a feeling, love is a choice."*

_____

_____

2: Do you know your love language and that of your family members? If so, think about how you demonstrate your love. Do you demonstrate love for them in your love language or theirs? Give an example:

_____

_____

_____

_____

3: Which of the 15 commitments in this chapter do you think is most important and why?

_____

_____

_____

_____

4: Which of the 15 commitments is lacking most in your family? How can you implement positive change in that area?

_____

_____

_____

_____

5: What can you do on a daily basis to show your family how much you love them?

_____

_____

_____

_____

06

connecting by

RESPECTING

"He who wants a rose must respect the thorn."

- Persian Proverb

As much as we would have liked everyone in our new family to accept and respect everyone else, unfortunately, that didn't happen. In reality, each individual had his or her own unique journey toward respecting each other. While each member of our family made the choice to love one another, growing to respect each other was another process altogether.

In our past, Roxanne and I had both experienced the pain and frustration of relationships void of healthy respect. Because of the emotional scars we had both suffered from our first marriages, we had made up our minds that

> **Respect, like love, is a choice. It seldom occurs sponaneously and often has to be earned.**

we would not tolerate disrespect in our home. It was extremely important to us to establish healthy boundaries for our marriage and for our children so that no one ever felt disrespected or dishonored. We knew that disrespect would severely damage the self-esteem of our children and create unhealthy barriers between our family members that could not be easily broken. We couldn't expect our children to respect us, them, or other people if we were disrespectful to them. Our highest goal was to set the standard for how to honor others in every circumstance.

Respect, like love, is a choice. It seldom occurs spontaneously and often has to be earned. Roxanne and I knew that if our children didn't respect or trust us, then they probably wouldn't obey us, either. If I wanted Roxanne's children to respect me as the new man of the house, I knew that I first needed to be worthy of their respect. That meant that I refused to say or do anything to them that I wouldn't want said or done to me. Their personal boundaries had to be every bit as important to me as my own, because crossing them would create fear, frustration, and distust in their hearts and eventually lead them to feel unloved as well. At times, choosing to be respectful was difficult. I knew that if I disrespected them in a moment of anger or frustration, I risked losing their trust, which is often difficult to rebuild. Our mutual respect kept us connected even when we didn't necessarily feel like being loving toward each other.

Our primary goal as parents was to create a safe and nurturing environment in which love could grow and flourish. We understood that respect was an essential element in that process. Like love, respect can be manifested through authenticity, consistency, humility, kindness, hard work, acceptance and patience. Just as individuals have different love languages, we also have different methods of gaining and giving respect. Those differences were clearly illustrated in the lives of our children.

Travis wrestled the most with our new family arrangement. As the oldest of Roxanne's children, he was closer to his biological father than Bobby or Tiffany. He stepped up to help his mom when his parents separated. My arrival on the scene left him feeling somewhat displaced, which made connecting quickly difficult. While he was never disrespectful, I could tell that he was stressed and torn about his loyalties. I understood his dilemma and eventually determined that what he really needed and longed for was a consistent example in his life. In his early years, he found it confusing and disillusioning when people proclaimed one thing with their words, yet, demonstrated the opposite message with their actions. Even in church he heard people preach against specific sins, he noticed that many of those same people went home and did the exact thing they had told him to avoid.

The last thing I wanted to be was another example of unreliability, so I made an honest effort to prove to Travis that he could count on me and trust my word. I was very careful to keep my promises to him and not to commit to anything that I couldn't deliver. I was surprised to find out, after two years, that the encouraging notes I left for the kids every morning had initially annoyed him. He told me that when I started leaving them, he threw them away because they made him mad. Later on, however, he was upset if I forgot to leave one. In spite of his initial response, he had grown to appreciate the thought behind those notes and realized that he actually enjoyed them. Travis gradually came to believe that I truly was a man of my word. Later on I got a glimpse of Travis's heart when my grandson, Jon, came to live with us. We suddenly went from three teenagers to four. Travis met me as I came in from work one evening and said, "Hey Roger, Jon can move into my room with me. That way he won't have to sleep on the couch and he will have a place to put his stuff." The kids' rooms were adequate, but small. I was afraid that putting two big teenage boys in one room would be a huge inconvenience to them both. Though I decided it would be too uncomfortable for them to room together, I recognized the sacrifice behind Travis's offer and greatly appreciated his unselfish gesture.

Bobby was a completely different challenge. He was acutely aware when people were phony and was disgusted by hypocrisy. Luckily, I've never been the type to put on a front, often struggling with the opposite problem—being too honest and blunt. He seemed to welcome and value my sense of transparency, which made it fairly easy for me to create a connection with him. Our respect for each other solidified when he and I attended a father-son retreat that his football coach held for the entire team. One of the exercises involved Bobby leading me blindfolded up a narrow mountain trail. He had to verbally direct me so that I avoided tripping over roots and rocks. When he took my blindfold off, I was standing on the edge of a cliff overlooking the beautiful valley below. My heart skipped a beat as I realized that if he had told me to take one more step forward, I would have fallen off the cliff and he would have been rid of his

stepfather. My esteem for him grew and I was quite thrilled that he had chosen not to get rid of me. I returned the favor by blindfolding him and leading him safely back down the hill.

We were also asked to write letters to each other and discuss them, giving us the opportunity to communicate personal feelings on a new level. In his letter he thanked me for all the support, love and dedication I had shown to his family. He shared how important it was to him that I tried to be an authentic role model for him and his siblings and how he felt blessed to have me in his life. I wrote that I loved him, was proud of him, and that I admired his hard work in school.

I also made sure he knew that I intended to stick around and that he could depend on me to be there for him. Over time, Bobby and Travis became the sons I never had.

Sensing that Tiffany longed for acceptance and appreciation, I jumped at the chance for us to attend a father-daughter seminar at our church. We spent a whole day listening to speakers and getting to know each other through various activities. We were able to talk about our feelings, fears, goals and visions for the future. She shared how she believed God was calling her to go to Thailand on a mission trip the following summer. I was impressed that though she couldn't even drive yet, she wanted to go on a mission trip to such a distant and unfamiliar location.

I assured Tiffany that I would pray with her about the trip, but I knew God was going to have a big job giving Roxanne and me peace about her going. As time went on, however, her passion for missions grew and God gave us peace about the trip to Thailand. To assure her of our support, Roxanne and I attended preparatory meetings for the team, helped her raise funds and prayed with her daily. We watched her confidence soar as we expressed our excitement about her trip and could see that she was validated by our encouragement.

Jon had a bit of an uphill battle when he moved in. While he and I had always been close and I knew he respected me, his real test was living with four new family members that he didn't know very well. Thankfully, the family responded to him in a way that quickly set him at ease. Roxanne was exactly what Jon needed—patient, kind, gentle and understanding.

From the beginning she loved him, talked with him and treated him like a son. He grew to appreciate her wisdom and tender spirit and easily respected her willing and faithful care towards him. Roxanne's love and hugs had a way of melting his fears and insecurities. Travis, Bobby and Tiffany acted like he belonged and treated him like a brother. In fact, they even listed him as a brother on their Facebook pages.

Because my two adult daughters never lived in the same house with our new family, the dynamic with them was a bit different. My oldest daughter, Lynn, took the cautious route, being very hesitant to draw close to Roxanne. Despite Lynn's skepticism, Roxanne humbly and consistently made the effort to show her that she cared, leaving the door open for them to have a closer connection in the future. For instance, every year she would buy Lynn a birthday present and delivered it to her doorstep, hoping that someday she would come around.

Lynn's real "ah-ha" moment came at her son, Jon's wedding. She told me that she finally realized that Roxanne was deeply loved by everyone she knew and that she was obviously a very special lady. She felt like she was missing out and wanted to get closer to Roxanne. After that, she not only made an effort to get to know Roxanne better, but also to have a closer relationship with me. Roxanne and I were elated and relieved that we were able to bond more deeply with her after that.

For my daughter, Casey, the bonding issue came up before our wedding when she and her three kids spent the night at my apartment. After tucking the kids into bed, she told me that she was bothered by the fact that Roxanne had three kids. I could tell that she was worried that my connection with Roxanne and her children would somehow diminish the bond I had with her and my three grandkids. As I tried to calm her fears, she asked pointedly, "Dad, how do you expect me to feel about this? What do you want me to do?" I was unsure of how to respond to her question.

When I awoke the next morning I had the answer. "Casey,

if something happened to Buddy and you remarried another guy with three kids, what would I do?"

She replied, "You would love them as if they were your own grandkids."

"You're absolutely right," I said, "and that's what I want you to do."

She tearfully responded, "I can do that Dad." And that's exactly what she did from then on.

Casey soon discovered Roxanne's loving and generous heart as she graciously drew Casey, Buddy and their children into our new family. To my amazement, the three grandkids instantly acknowledged Roxanne, as Grandma, making it easy for her to embrace them as her own. Eventually, Casey also got to know Roxanne's children and came to love them as if they were her own flesh and blood.

Person by person, our family was woven together like a beautiful tapestry, each color and texture complementing the others. In the process of attempting to connect, we learned that each person grows to respect others at their own rate. Roxanne and I tried to let bonding happen at their pace rather than ours. Some took months and others took years, but the consistency we established by making loving choices eventually won their respect.

Unfortunately, there may be times when you strive to esteem someone in every possible way, yet, the person chooses not to reciprocate. Regardless of their response, we knew that if we continued to walk the path of integrity and respect the personal boundaries of others, we were creating an open door for each person to enter in their own time. By waiting on God to do the work in the resistant individuals, there was less stress and more peace in our household. While we were waiting, God also had an opportunity to work in all of us to develop patience, unconditional love, a deeper prayer life and a total dependence on Him for the outcome.

POINTS 2 PONDER
ROAD to respect ▸ >>

1: How and why is respect so important in family relationships?

_____

_____

_____

_____

2: Which do you feel is more important to you: love or respect? Why?

_____

_____

_____

_____

3: How do you think you earn respect from another person?

_____

_____

_____

_____

07

you have not because you

ASK NOT

"The best way to prepare yourself for your own miracle is to rejoice in someone elses."

- Bill Johnson

With the addition of Jon to our family, our perfect home, which we bought just 18 months before, suddenly became too small. It was obvious that we needed a bigger house. This would be a huge undertaking, since securing our first home was a miracle in its own right. Fortunately, I learned long ago that God can and will do things that we can't even imagine if we simply ask.

Over the 15 years prior to our marriage, I had taught several hundred financial seminars in churches, businesses and schools. As a financial counselor with a strong call to ministry, I did a considerable amount of debt and budget counseling. Occasionally, I also ended up doing marriage counseling by default. The majority of the people that I counseled primarily had two financial problems: they spent more than they earned and they didn't have an established plan for their finances.

To nudge them in the right direction, I challenged them to pray about making two commitments that could change their lives forever. The first was to refrain from going into debt for any reason other than purchasing a home. The second was to commit to a written spending plan and stick to it. I knew that if they made those key commitments, they could eventually eliminate their financial problems, prevent further disputes over money and reach their life goals. It was my practice to close every meeting with prayer, asking God to intervene in the area of their finances.

To my surprise, God seemed to bless those prayers by showing off a bit. There were countless occasions where He seemed to take specific prayers as His cue to make a grand entrance into the lives of my clients. It was incredible to witness how quickly and precisely He answered many of those prayers, from the small and simple to the grand and outrageous.

One morning during a budget meeting, a young couple requested that I add a payment to their spending plan to buy a new range since theirs no longer worked. Upon reviewing their plan, I determined that their budget was already tight and would simply not allow for a monthly payment. I asked the couple, "Why don't you just ask God to provide for your need? Would you wait for a few weeks and ask Him to provide you one so you don't have to go into debt?"

The wife looked at me like I was insane and retorted, "Is God in the business of providing stoves?"

I answered, "Do you need a replacement stove?" She nodded. "Do you have the money to buy one?" I asked.

"No," she replied.

"Then yes, God provides stoves. Philippians 4:19 says, 'My God will meet all your needs according to the riches of His glory in Christ Jesus.'"

Finally, she agreed to wait and pray. Only two hours later she called me back with this story. "After our visit, I went home and told my friend that I had just met with this crazy financial counselor who said that I shouldn't buy a stove on credit. Instead he suggested that I ask God to provide me one. Would you pray with me about that?"

Her friend replied, "Yes, but, in the meantime, come over and get the one in our garage. It still works well, but we don't need it. You are welcome to have it."

God's method of provision was pretty impressive to both of us, but the story gets better. I decided to share that tale with a church in Dallas, Texas, during a kick-off session for one of my financial seminars. After the service, one of the ladies raced over to her friend and confessed, "I think God was speaking to me through that story. We were going to go this afternoon to buy a new stove on credit. I think I am supposed to wait and pray for one instead. Would you pray with me about that?" To her surprise, her friend replied, "It so happens that I, too, have an extra one in my garage and it's yours if you want it."

I told that story many more times and many who heard it also gained the courage to test God's promise of provision.

One morning during an emergency budget meeting, a couple informed me that their refrigerator had gone out the previous night and all their food was ruined. They had already made the commitment not to go into debt, but saw no other way to get a new fridge. I almost felt guilty telling them to get an ice chest for a few days and trust God to meet their need. Before they left, I prayed with them for God to provide.

As they were leaving my conference room, the people in the waiting room next door stepped out and said, "We overheard you praying and we believe God wants us to meet your need. We just bought a new refrigerator, but our old one still works perfectly and it's sitting in our garage. You are more than welcome to have it."

God had done it again, meeting specific needs in mere minutes. My goal in sharing these stories is not to present God as a servant boy whose job is to provide whatever you need whenever you need it, but to impart faith. He clearly delights in those who trust Him and call on Him in their hour of need. The simple act of asking and trusting Him

> **Nothing is more fun than seeing God answer with a mircaculous, "yes." Yet, I think we may grow and learn more about God when He answers with the less popular, "no" or "wait."**

actually prompts Him to answer. If you ask me, I think He gets a kick out of being able to shock us with His ability to give us exactly what we need in the most unpredictable ways possible.

As I share my stories of the power of prayer, it may seem as if God answered all our prayers with a resounding, "yes." I wish that were true, because nothing is more fun than seeing God answer with a miraculous, "yes." Yet, I think we may grow and learn more about God when He answers with the less popular, "no" or "wait." We had our share of all three answers, but we were confident that God always heard and always answered. Often when He said, "no," or "wait," He had something even better for us than what we had requested. For example, when my financial business initially started to expand, we outgrew our first office fairly quickly and I started praying for a bigger office. I found what I believed was the perfect office and location and made what I thought was a very reasonable offer.

To my dismay, my offer was declined. I asked God to give me favor with the owners so that they would accept my next offer. Then, I submitted a higher offer. It was the maximum I could pay at that time. Again they refused. I accepted that God had said, "no," or at least, "wait," so I stopped searching for another office. Knowing that it is often the, "no" or "wait" that prompts one to doubt God's faithfulness and miss seeing His blessings in disguise, I decided not to doubt. Instead, I chose to believe that He simply had a better plan than I did.

A year later, we found ourselves feeling more and more like sardines. The office got so overcrowded that our UPS man couldn't even deliver a box without causing a disastrous traffic jam. In frustration, I went outside to get some air and again began to ask God for a larger office. I told the Lord, "You have to do something! I don't even have room to walk in my own office!" After standing there for a few moments, I heard a little voice say, "That office you tried to buy is still for sale." Out of curiosity, I jumped into my truck and decided to go see for myself. To my surprise, the same exact real estate sign was still posted in the front of the building.

I quickly picked up the phone and called the realtor. He remembered me and said that the owners had dropped the price to much less than I had originally offered. By waiting a year, I was able to purchase that office for 25 percent less than my initial offer. God answered my prayer at just the right time, taught me a lesson on patience, and gave me a discount in the process.

I could fill this book with stories of God's faithfulness and provision in the lives of the people I met and prayed with over those years, so asking for a bigger house for our expanding family did not seem too crazy. We had very limited resources at that time and bigger houses were certainly in demand. The real estate market in our area was very strong, which made me a bit hesitant to put a "For Sale" sign in our yard. I worried that if we sold our home, we wouldn't be able to afford the five-bedroom house we needed. That same day, Roxanne and I got on our knees and asked God for a buyer for our house and a new home large enough for our big family. It was extremely important for us to get an affordable home without breaking our commitment to refrain from debt.

Less than 24 hours later, God was already at work answering our prayer. Roxanne told me about a sign she saw on a trip to the lake that advertised a five-bedroom home for sale by a realtor that we knew. After calling her and viewing the house that afternoon, we learned that the realtor went to church with the owners and knew them personally. The house was perfect for us and the owners were hoping to move to a smaller home, because their kids were going off to college soon. Since they needed to downsize and my family needed to upsize, I threw out the crazy idea of a house swap. I thought the chances were slim, but I knew that no job would be too big for my God.

After looking at our house the next day, they told us that they were equally interested in a switch. I offered to trade homes and pay them all the money I could pull together at that time. To our surprise and delight, they accepted the offer and we scheduled a January 15, 2006, move day. God answered our prayer for a bigger house and their prayer for a smaller one in record time.

We were left with yet another problem. The house we were moving into desperately needed painting inside and out, as well as some other repair work. Our kids loved the house, but the previous owners were an artistic family. They had painted gigantic airplanes, gothic looking creatures, cars and monster trucks on the walls throughout the house. Our kids were not anxious to move in without painting, so we began to pray for the money to take care of painting and minor repairs.

Just a few days before the closing, Roxanne got a call from

her attorney. She learned that her insurance company had finally settled a claim from a car accident that had occurred several years before and she would be receiving a check in the next few days. She told me how she had prayed for that settlement many times over the years and had finally decided that God was saying, "no." In His divine wisdom and perfect timing, God miraculously provided the money for painting and repairs.

The kids all invited their friends over for painting parties to paint their rooms. Tiffany's group got a little carried away and had to start over. Nevertheless, within a few weeks we were totally settled and it finally felt like our home.

We made many wonderful memories in that house. We lived only a few miles from Beaver Lake, so we spent hundreds of hours boating, water skiing, wakeboarding, and tubing as a family. We regularly went hiking, fishing, picnicking and camping at the park by the lake. Roxanne absolutely loved packing a picnic and spending the day floating on a raft with the whole family.

Over the years we developed a number of family traditions, but none was more important than praying together about our needs, our family, our friends and our blessings. We witnessed God doing many things in direct response to our prayers. When each of our kids turned 16, we prayed for a good car that we could purchase with cash and which would last them for a long time. God answered our prayers every time. In fact, we're still driving most of those cars today. He didn't just give us something to scrape by with for a few years. Instead, He blessed us with quality cars that would run for years to come.

Often, we are like children who think that candy would make a great dinner. We tell them, "no," but that usually doesn't make them very happy. Yet, as those children grow up, they understand why, "no" or "wait" was the right answer. Every time we prayed and trusted in God's plan, He proved to us that He really cares for our every need, and He wants to show us what He can do.

POINTS 2 PONDER
PRAYING for your family's NEEDS ›

1: Describe where prayer fits into your family life:

_____

_____

_____

_____

2: What needs are in your life now that you haven't prayed about?

_____

_____

_____

_____

3: Describe a time when God answered one of your prayers with a, "no" or "wait." What did you learn during that experience?

_____

_____

_____

_____

4: What prayer habits would you like to establish in your home?

_____

_____

_____

_____

_____

_____

08

a call to
HAITI

"It is a divine cooperation to fulfill your life's destiny. When we are willing, God moves, opens doors, and shows us the way. Then we must follow, work, and make sacrifices. All the while God is there supplying what we lack."

- Abigail Skinner

The years flew by, filled with football and basketball games, driving lessons, family vacations, mission trips and church activities. As our family bond grew stronger, we created several new family traditions. We had big family birthday celebrations, decorated the Christmas tree after Thanksgiving dinner, and attended Christmas Eve services together. We often had game nights, and went on vacation together at least once a year.

Then, before we knew it, all the kids had finished high school and moved out. That left us with a house far too big for only two people. Without the kids around, it seemed empty and didn't feel like home anymore. We began praying and searching for a smaller house closer to my office. After almost a year of searching, we finally found a home we loved where we planned to stay for the rest of our lives. To commemorate our new home, we bought a concrete bench engraved with our names and anniversary date. We placed it in our back yard under our wedding arch, which had been in storage for several years. Many enjoyable evenings were spent sitting on that bench talking and watching the sun go down. We were more than eager to begin the next stage in our journey and were elated that we had found the perfect place to spend it.

As empty nesters, Roxanne and I began looking for activities that did not focus on the children. Early in December, 2009, while looking for a Christmas present for Roxanne, I stumbled onto a last minute cruise deal that was almost too good to be true. The ship would leave port on New Year's Day and it included nine full days in the Caribbean. Only three weeks later, we found ourselves celebrating New Year's Eve in a beautiful hotel in Miami. At midnight, we watched incredible fireworks explode over the Blue Lagoon, anxious to board our ship the next morning. It was magical.

Checking in at the cruise terminal the next day, we were delighted to learn that we had been upgraded to a balcony room at no charge. Roxanne was ecstatic, she had always wanted to experience a cruise in a balcony room. Since our first day was a sea day, we spent the day relaxing and exploring the different attractions onboard. We got a couples massage, ate dinner in the formal dining room, and watched a Russian acrobat show. We were instantly hooked on the cruise experience.

The ship's first scheduled stop was Samana, Dominican Republic. The next morning, as we were eating breakfast on our balcony, we noticed we were cruising alongside a very large landmass.

Roxanne asked, "Babe, what island do you think that is?"

"I think that is probably Haiti," I replied. "Haiti and the Dominican Republic share an island. Since we are stopping at Samana today, we would have to sail around Haiti to get to that side of the Dominican Republic."

"That is Haiti?" Roxanne blurted out as she burst into tears. "I had no idea we would pass Haiti!" She then explained, "Babe, I know beyond a shadow of a doubt that God has given me a burden to go there someday."

As she continued to cry, all I could say was, "I believe you will." Through her tears, she watched as Haiti faded into the distance. She almost looked homesick, as if Haiti was her true homeland. I found it curious that she seemed so attached to a place she had never visited, but I also knew that God often softens our hearts for specific ministries. As we silently watched Haiti disappear from view, I wrapped my arms around her. My mind drifted back to an earlier conversation in which Roxanne first shared her tender spirit toward the Haitian people.

Haiti first captured her heart when she was only 8-years-old. She grew up in a humble family with two older and two younger sisters. Her father was a holiness preacher in a small country church in southern Missouri. For a few years, her three cousins lived with them, making their financial situation quite difficult. One summer, all the kids were planning to go to church camp, but the cost was $20 per child. All the kids were required to raise their own money for camp. Roxanne worked very hard and managed to save $10.

One Sunday evening a missionary from Haiti came to her church to share about his work there. Like many missionaries, he displayed slides that depicted the poverty many Haitians endured. As Roxanne watched the slideshow, her heart broke for the Haitian people.

She started to cry and told her mom, "I want to give my $10 to that missionary." Her mom whispered back, "You shouldn't give away your money for camp." Through her tears, Roxanne continued to insist that she wanted to help the missionary. Noticing the commotion, her father slipped in beside her and asked what was going on. After hearing what she wanted to do, he said, "If you donate your money, you will not be able to go to camp."

"I understand that, Daddy." she explained, "I would rather give it to Haiti and stay home from camp." Undeterred by the consequences, her father let her give her $10 to the Haitian missionary. Because of her sacrifice, she was the only child in her family who did not go to camp that year. From that day forward, Roxanne had a burden for the country of Haiti.

We stopped at several islands during the remainder of our cruise and had a wonderful time, but Roxanne just couldn't get Haiti off her mind. She talked about it constantly. We were discussing attending an on-board lecture on Haiti's history when we heard a strange voice, which sounded like it was coming from the empty chair beside us.

"If you can hear me, pick this up," it chimed. Looking around to see where the voice was coming from, we spotted a walkie-talkie lying in the chair at our table.

Roxanne picked it up saying, "Hello?" Minutes later, a couple showed up to retrieve the walkie-talkie and introduced themselves as Gail and Sheila.

Remarkably, they lived in Springfield, Missouri, just two hours north of our home. We really hit it off with them and a friendship quickly developed. One evening during dinner, Roxanne shared her burden for Haiti, explaining the emotion she felt as we had passed Haiti a few days before and how it had rekindled her desire to go there someday. None of us could have imagined the journey that lay before us because of that chance meeting.

Our ship docked back in Miami on January 10, 2010. Two days later, a massive earthquake hit Haiti that ultimately killed 316,000 people, injured another 300,000 and left one million homeless. Roxanne was glued to the television, watching reports of rescue workers digging people out of the rubble. She trembled and cried as she watched people being buried in mass graves, children being left with no parents and everyone living in terror of the next aftershock. When I got home from work on January 14, Roxanne met me at the door. The first words out of her mouth were, "Babe, what would you say if I told you I wanted to help with the Haiti relief efforts?"

"I know you have a huge burden for Haiti," I replied. "I sincerely have no problem with you going, but I think the timing is wrong. Right now they need rescue workers to dig people out of the rubble and haul bodies to makeshift morgues. I don't feel confident that you will be safe or comfortable with that kind of work. I suggest that you wait a few months until this phase is over and then plan to go."

A few months later Roxanne learned that a local church was taking a team to Haiti. We attended the introductory meeting where they laid out the plans for the trip. Throughout the meeting, Roxanne quietly cried. On the way home she said, "Babe, you do not need to feel like you should go on this trip, but I have to go." With a tiny bit of terror in my heart I replied, "I know you do." From that day forward she began attending training sessions with the group that would be leaving for Haiti that year at the end of July.

Roxanne might have been consumed by thoughts of her upcoming trip, but then Travis made an announcement that momentarily redirected her excitement. He had been dating Elise for several months and they seemed to be getting pretty serious. When he first brought her to meet us, we were skeptical since she was older than Travis and had three daughters from her previous marriage. However, our

concerns quickly melted away as we fell in love with Elise and her children. As we grew to love them, Travis declared their official engagement and asked to be married in our backyard under our wedding arch. Roxanne was especially elated since Travis would be the first of her children to marry. Not long after the announcement, Roxanne was busy planning a wedding scheduled just three weeks before she planned to leave for Haiti.

The wedding was picturesque. As He had for Roxanne and I, God held back the forecasted rain until the ceremony was over. The whole event, including the threatening storm, was a déjà vu experience for us, reminding us of God's goodness at our own wedding. The highlight of the evening was when Travis got to dance

with his mom to "The Perfect Fan" by the Backstreet Boys. Roxanne beamed as tears ran down Travis' face. It was a moment neither of them would ever forget. Hours of laughing, storytelling and picture taking followed. Then the guests formed a receiving line and lit up the night with sparklers as Travis and Elise headed off to their honeymoon. "There goes my baby," Roxanne said as they drove away. I could tell she was getting sentimental, so I gave her a big hug and suggested that we call it a night.

We gathered up our new grandkids, Audrey, Natalie and Susie. They stayed with us while Travis and Elise were on their honeymoon and we had loads of fun getting to know each other. Elise and her three daughters fit into our family like puzzle pieces we never knew were missing. Roxanne and I thought we couldn't be happier, but then, we got another delightful surprise that proved us wrong. Not long after the wedding, Travis and Elise informed us they had prayerfully decided to have a child together. That would require Elise to have a tubal reversal, which they planned to do in the very near future. Roxanne was overjoyed about the prospect of her first grandchild. Life was almost too good to be true.

After helping Travis and Elise get settled into their new home together, our attention returned to Roxanne's impending trip to Haiti. In spite of my male ego screaming that I couldn't let my wife go to Haiti alone, I knew God was not calling me to go. Instead, I helped her gather all the things she would need for her trip, assisted the team in packing dozens of bags filled with clothes and shoes and drove her to the airport on July 30, 2010, to depart for Haiti. Driving away from the airport, I had a huge empty feeling inside, mingled with a divine peace that God was going to take care of her.

Although the team arrived safely at the airport in Port-au-Prince, my faith was tested by the text messages she sent on the trip to the mission. They had barely loaded all the bags on the bus when a horrific rainstorm began. The roads in Haiti are like rocky creek beds in dry conditions and like flooded creeks when it's raining. As they drove through Port-au-Prince, Roxanne described the piles of rubble that once were buildings.

I sensed her shock as she depicted the tent city that came up to the edge of the road and extended as far as the eye could see. Dozens of children were standing right by the road, being soaked in the pouring rain. Sadly, many of the tents were nothing more than sheets stretched over wooden poles.

The traffic was horrible and there was about a foot of water rushing over the road. The old bus they were riding in had no air conditioning and one of the Haitians from the mission was holding two wires together to keep the windshield wipers working. The 20-mile trip to the JoyHouse mission took four and a half hours. They arrived just before dark, which was a big concern because Haiti is not a safe place after sundown. Needless to say, that was an intense time for everyone involved.

Roxanne called me the next morning from the roof of JoyHouse. She had shivered through a cold shower and sweated profusely throughout the night as she slept on the top bunk. Breakfast consisted of fried spam, fresh avocado and instant coffee. I could hear the excitement in her voice as she talked about starting the day's work.

She spent part of the next seven days putting together the small vinyl houses provided by Samaritan's Purse. The houses were about the size of my small tool shed, yet the people were thrilled to get one. While the team was putting one of the houses together, Roxanne walked outside to the back of the house. A Haitian woman was there with her hands in the air, praising God in Creole for her tiny one room house. She couldn't speak English and Roxanne couldn't speak Creole, but they embraced in a hug that said it all.

When she wasn't working on the makeshift houses, she was distributing clothing, shoes and hygiene kits. There were huge smiles and warm, sweaty hugs as mothers picked out clothes to take home to their children. One young boy was so elated over his pink flip-flops and matching pink top that he modeled them for all his friends. Roxanne got a kick out of the teenage girl wearing a shirt that said, "My mother warned me about California guys."

"They don't care what it says or what color it is," explained Roxanne, "They're just happy to have it." Children would stand in line for an hour to get a hygiene kit with a toothbrush, toothpaste, a bar of soap, a washcloth and a small bottle of hand sanitizer. She said, "They walked away with the biggest smiles on their faces. You'd think I had just given them a big bag of Halloween candy."

On a visit to an orphanage, the mission team brought clothes and shoes for each child and helped them find items that fit. While the children listened to a Bible story, Roxanne sat on a wooden bench nearby. Halfway into the story, a little boy came and nestled in her lap and fell asleep.

The next day was Sunday. Roxanne made her way to the makeshift tent that served as a replacement for the church that had collapsed during the earthquake. She was choking back tears as she told me more about that service. As she sat down on one of the rough wooden benches, she noticed a group of children walking down the hill from the orphanage. That same toddler saw her again, crawled up in her lap and slept the entire service.

Roxanne was amazed at hearing many familiar hymns sung in Creole as the people worshiped. When the service ended, one of the older children from the orphanage motioned for Roxanne to put the little boy down. She tearfully watched him climb back up the hill to the orphanage.

The extreme heat, lack of hot water, unpredictable electrical power and minimal food made the circumstances inconvenient for Roxanne and the other workers, but that didn't bother her. Regardless of the hardships, she loved every minute she was there. It broke her heart to see the struggles that the

Haitians faced, especially after such a massive natural disaster. Her sense of calling to Haiti was unquestionable, and she was determined to help even after her challenging first visit.

When Roxanne arrived back in Tulsa, I watched her beaming as she walked down the airport corridor toward me. In spite of her less than fragrant aroma, I embraced her, happy to have her back in my arms. Neither the bus she rode back in, nor the airport had air conditioning and she was not able to wash her clothes the entire time she was there. That odor was, however, a small price to pay for the blessing of having her back and knowing she had fulfilled her childhood dream. Her first words to me were, "I love you," followed by, "I can't wait to go back."

While JoyHouse had been spared any major damage in the earthquake, the church next door had totally collapsed. Roxanne came home with a burning desire to raise the money to rebuild that church. She sent letters to everyone she knew with a picture of the tent they were using for church. She made phone calls to friends, family and local businesses, and talked to nearly everyone she met about the need in Haiti. Our new friends, Gail and Sheila, and many other friends and family made contributions. With their support, Roxanne quickly raised enough money to pour the foundation and the floor. She was so passionate about the project that, within a few months, she raised the funds necessary to enable local Haitians and mission teams to completely rebuild the church. All of this served only to fan the flame of the burden of love she carried.

Norma, the leader of JoyHouse, recognized the unusual passion Roxanne had for the Haitian people and asked her if she could come back to Haiti in September to help with a special project they were planning. I admit that I was not excited about her going back within two months of her first trip, yet her enthusiasm was contagious. In my heart I knew God was saying, "It will be okay."

The special project, called "The Joyful Weddings" was quite interesting. For a couple to legitimately marry within the Haitian culture, they had to be able to have a wedding and a reception where they fed their guests. Since very few Haitian couples had enough money to feed 40 or 50 people, they often just lived together and never got married. That presented yet another problem. If they were not legally married, they could still attend church, but weren't allowed to become members or be baptized.

The plan was for Roxanne to bring donated wedding dresses, suits, shoes and low cost wedding rings from the US to Haiti. There were four couples from the JoyHouse church at that time that wanted to get married. Not only did Roxanne bring in all the wedding clothing, she fitted the brides, helped them with hair and makeup and served at the reception. They had four back-to-back ceremonies and fed 200 guests at JoyHouse. The whole event went very well and the couples were profoundly thankful. The Joyful Weddings might seem like an odd ministry, yet the reports from the community were priceless. The locals said that they were not so surprised by the provision of food, fresh water, clothing and housing after the earthquake, but they saw The Joyful Weddings as a true gift of love. Going far above and beyond meeting their basic physical needs, the project provided for their emotional and spiritual needs.

Roxanne made her third trip to Haiti in April 2011. Her passion and love for the Haitian people had so impressed Matthew, one

of the interpreters at JoyHouse, that his fiancé asked Roxanne to be her matron of honor. Of course, she happily accepted. The wedding was held in the home of the bride's parents, so Roxanne was able to see and interact with Haitians in a whole new setting. She was delighted to be involved in such an important ceremony in Haitian culture.

Even though she couldn't understand a word they said, her heart overflowed with joy just to be in their presence.

After Roxanne had taken three trips in less than a year, Norma asked her to start training future groups that would be going to Haiti. Her first training assignment was at my daughter, Casey's church in Neosho, Missouri. Casey's husband, Buddy, is the pastor there and Roxanne's passion for Haiti had lit a fire in both their hearts.

The Neosho team made their first trip to Haiti in July, 2011. When Roxanne and I met the team at the airport upon their return she spoke extensively with every team member. The group was so excited about the trip that they had already planned another one for February, 2012. That team, which included our daughter Tiffany, facilitated 12 Joyful Weddings, as well as other projects.

It appears that Roxanne's passion for Haiti has taken root in Casey. She resigned from her job as a math teacher and has since led several mission trips to Haiti to work with JoyHouse. Her three children Jarvis, Carson and Riley have now visited Haiti as well.

The church that was destroyed in the earthquake initially held about 150 people. It has since been rebuilt with a capacity of 350 and has full attendance nearly every week. Thirty-five years ago, a little girl in a small country church sacrificed $10 and a trip to camp, and God gave her a vision of someday making a difference in Haiti. Roxanne is proof that God can use just one obscure person, no matter how old or how young, to influence hundreds of lives in a positive way. It is never too early or too late to follow the call. As of today, her dream has impacted hundreds of people both in Haiti and the United States and will continue as God expands her influence.

POINTS2PONDER
LIFE mission ▸»

1: How would you describe your purpose in life?

_____

_____

_____

_____

2: Have you pursued and followed God's will for your life? If not, what practical things can you do to discover His will for you?

_____

_____

_____

_____

3: Have you ever felt called to help a particular people group? How have you responded to that call?

_____

_____

_____

_____

4: What fears prevent you from fulfilling God's plan for your life?

_____

_____

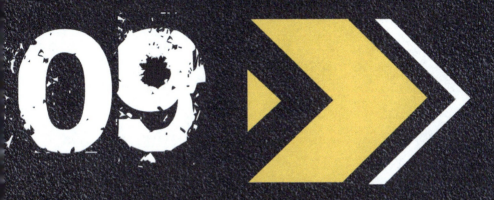

09

change in the
AIR

"**If you start the day reading the obituaries, you live your day a little differently.**"

- David Leithan, *Love Is the Higher Law*

At the onset of 2011, Roxanne was still heavily involved in her new ministry. I had owned my own financial services business for almost 22 years, serving as both a client representative and visionary for the company. I daily sought God's will for the business and it was almost always clear to me what direction God was taking us.

Several years before, it had become evident to me that God was blessing and expanding the business. I added two partners to aid me in taking care of our surplus of clients. I felt profoundly responsible for my employees, partners, and the financial future of our clients. Having more than a few people depending on me gave new meaning to the word, responsibility.

For the most part, I always loved my job and I awoke every Monday morning anxious to get to work. In early 2011, my priorities seemed to be shifting. My passion for the business was waning. It was as if God had pulled the curtains over my eyes. My ability to see His short-term and long-term plans for the business was blocked. Just as God had called Roxanne to Haiti, I began to believe that God was calling me to a specific ministry that was yet to be revealed.

I have always been a creature of habit, thus I was terrified at the thought of such a radical change. One of my better habits is my morning routine. I have been praying, reading the Bible and journaling every morning for the last 28 years. I learned long ago how powerful it is to be able to look back on any given day of my life and read the details I recorded about it. I have often documented events that I never would have remembered and answers to prayers I had forgotten I had prayed. Even the ability to accurately write this book comes from the pages of my journal. Here are a few clips from my journal in early 2011 that stunned me as I read them.

2-16-2011: *Lord, I was sure I would finish my days out right here, but I have no vision. I feel like a guy with his nose against the wall. I can't see. I have this weird feeling that you have something else for me to do.*

3-22-2011: *God, what do you want me to do the rest of my life? I sense a change, but I don't know what. How can I be so silly to think that the God of the universe can have a distinct plan for an almost 61-year-old man in a huge world of turmoil? Yet, I do. Wow, Lord. I am listening. I will follow.*

As I felt my interest in business slipping away, I developed an overwhelming desire to spend as much time with Roxanne as possible. In March, I began to think about taking a cruise to celebrate our April birthdays and our seventh wedding anniversary coming up in May. I came across an 18-day transatlantic cruise that was amazingly economical. Normally I would not have considered it because of the length of time I would have to be away from work. However, my first thought that day was, "If I am able to use air miles for free flights, we're going."

Within an hour, I had found flights that I could secure with my air miles and I signed us up for the cruise. Roxanne had always wanted to take a cruise to Europe, and I could not pass up the deal. Even though it was a stretch financially and rather scary being away that long, I honestly had the impression that God was saying, "Do it."

The entire month leading up to the cruise was exhausting. We worked so hard trying to get everything done before we left that we crashed as soon as we arrived at the hotel in Fort Lauderdale. When we walked onto that ship the next day, I felt my mind reformat. My fears and doubts melted away and for the next 19 days we didn't worry about the business, the kids, the house, or any of our other responsibilities. For the first time in years, it seemed that God had freed me both mentally and physically from my day-to-day duties. I was able to take pleasure in the small things rather than focusing on the big picture.

With that freedom came the ability to concentrate on Roxanne and enjoy the amazing trip. It included eight stops in seven countries and nine days at sea. We laughed, talked, danced and relaxed more than either of us ever had in our entire lives. We enjoyed breathtaking scenery, walked miles and held hands for hours on end. Before long we were absolutely unaware of the time or even what day of the week it was.

Standing on the deck early one morning, Roxanne looked deep into my eyes and said, "Thank you so much for this trip. I never thought I would be able to take a trip like this." I responded, "You know what, Babe? I never thought I'd take this much time off work all at once, but I'm sure glad I did. It has been the best trip of my life." The entire trip was truly a gift from God.

I returned to work renewed, refreshed and revived. I hoped that I would hit the ground running and be excited to be back on track. I quickly realized I had simply lost all enthusiasm for my work. I began praying, *Lord, what do I need to do now?*

His answer came through a series of strange events. God first got my attention on May 22, 2011, when Roxanne had to go to Neosho, Missouri, for a Haiti training meeting at Buddy and Casey's church. I decided to go along and take my three grandkids out for dinner. As they jumped into the car, I asked them where they wanted to eat. "Billy Sims BBQ!" they all shouted in unison. Billy Sims was in Joplin, Missouri, about 20 miles north of Neosho. Normally, I would have said no way because of the distance, but that night I thought, why not? As we walked into the restaurant half an hour later, everyone seemed to be watching the television nervously. Our waitress informed us that we were under a tornado watch and asked if we still wanted to order. We decided to stay and sat down with the tornado siren screaming outside. While we waited, I kept my eyes on the weather forecaster as he tracked the storm. The report showed clear skies to the south. We had driven right into the most dangerous part of the storm track.

Riley asked, "Pop, are you scared?"

I answered, "No, Riley. 'What time I am afraid, I will trust in Him.' Jesus is with us and He will take care of us."

"My mom always says that!" she spurted.

"That's because I used to tell her that when she had a bad dream as a little girl."

As we left the restaurant, I overheard the manager talking about closing early due to the tornado warning and he told us to be safe. Looking to the west, I saw the blackened sky and the clouds appeared to be on the ground. I decided to return to Neosho, since the weather report showed the storm moving in the opposite direction. Heading east down 7th Street, I could see the threatening tempest in my rear view mirror.

The light turned red as we approached Rangeline Road and we were startled by another sudden screech of the tornado siren. A wave of anxiety swept over me and I was overwhelmed with temptation to turn right onto Rangeline, which would have taken me to Neosho. However, a voice within my spirit clearly told me to stay east on 7th Street. Opting to wait for a green light, I continued east on 7th and headed toward the Highway 71 bypass, an alternate route to Neosho. Unfortunately, I got so distracted watching the storm in my mirror that I missed my turn onto the 71 bypass.

We made a quick U-turn onto the ramp as the menacing clouds closed in on us. I sped down the bypass toward Neosho and saw a highway patrol car headed toward Joplin with lights flashing, followed by two more patrol cars a few minutes later. I was relieved to escape what appeared to be the heart of the storm. Buddy met us at the door of the church and the kids excitedly relayed the story of how we had outrun the storm. The color drained from his face and I thought he was going to pass out. When he regained his composure, he told us that during the meeting, one of the ladies on the Haiti team had received a call from her sister in Joplin. She called from her basement to tell them that her house had been blown away and she was unsure if she would be able get out of the rubble. They had stopped the meeting to pray for her and the city of Joplin as the EF5 multiple vortex tornado destroyed everything in its path.

As Roxanne and I headed home a bit shaken, she received a call from her sister, Sandra, telling us that she was in Joplin when the storm hit and had taken cover in a service station on 7th Street which we had passed on our way out of town. She had barely reached safety when she heard the storm ripping the buildings apart outside. When she finally came out, she counted 10 semi-trucks turned upside down. Driving to Joplin High School, where she was employed as principal, she discovered that the school and all the surrounding homes had been destroyed. St. John's Hospital was badly damaged and injured people were wandering the streets with no place to go. In shock and uncertain of what to do, Sandra began using her van to transport injured people to a makeshift emergency medical center. The realization that we had probably passed her going the opposite direction on 7th Street sent a chill down my spine. We had missed the most destructive part of the storm by mere minutes.

The next morning, Roxanne and I flew out for a business meeting in Denver, Colorado. When we got to the hotel, I was glued to the TV footage of the tornado. They repeatedly ran a clip that looked identical to what I had seen in my rear view mirror the night before. It seemed as if the cameraman was shooting that video from my backseat. It occurred to me that without realizing it, I had watched the storm destroying the city as I drove away the previous night. Had I turned right onto Rangeline Road as I had momentarily considered, we would have driven right into the eye of the storm.

The menacing twister completely demolished everything for more than a mile on Rangeline Road, just three miles south of the intersection where I had decided to go straight. At least 2,000 buildings and homes were obliterated. People were still trapped in their homes, 116 were dead and many more were missing. I fell to my knees crying, "Thank You, Lord, for sparing us. What do I need to see and learn from this experience?"

Roxanne and I tried to enjoy ourselves in Denver, but the trip was overshadowed by the disturbing news from Joplin. Listening to the grim reports of the dead, injured and missing weighed heavily on both our hearts. As we headed home, I still couldn't get my mind off the fact that I had just barely escaped death by tornado.

Only days after being home, I began to experience chest pains. I called my cardiologist who had placed two stents in my heart back in 2002. After examining me, he scheduled a cardiac catheterization procedure for the next day. My journal entries from the first few days of June expressed what was going on in my mind at that time.

6-2-2011: *I was surprised that my heart cath looked normal. There is no blockage and the stents looked clear. In the last ten days I missed a tornado by three minutes and had a blockage-free heart cath after having pretty severe chest pains. Thank you, Lord.*

6-3-2011: *Lord, you've spared me twice in the last eleven days. You have my full attention. What are you saying to me? Do you have something else for me to do?*

6-5-2011: *Lord, Roxanne's childhood friend who spent the night with us just two months ago was killed in a bicycle wreck yesterday. The last two weeks have brought the uncertainties of life right into our faces. It makes me want to live every day knowing it could be my last. Lord, I want to finish well.*

6-7-2011: *This morning my partner, Kevin, shared that he woke up at 2 AM and was compelled to read the book of Joshua. As he read about Moses dying and Joshua assuming leadership, he felt like God was saying to him, "Roger may be the first guy to leave the business. You need to step up and be ready to take the lead." I told him that I feel like God is doing something big in my life, but I'm not sure what.*

6-10-2011: *Good morning, Lord. Elise is having her tubal reversal today. I hope I live long enough to see them have a baby.*

Over the next couple of weeks I continued to have spells with dizziness, lightheadedness and chest pain. Fearing that I might be having a heart attack, I made two trips to the emergency room. I thought about my family medical history as I waited for the doctor. My father passed away in his sleep from a heart attack when he was only 44. I was also reminded that my grandfather, at age 44, had raced to the hospital with chest pains and died moments later. Even though I was well past the age of 44, I couldn't help but be worried that I might suffer the same sudden fate.

I shuddered to think of how unprepared my partners would be if I were to die unexpectedly. The thought was eye opening. In that moment, I determined that if I were able to go back to work, I would start making arrangements for that possibility immediately. I cared about them too much to take a chance at leaving them with my loose ends. I wanted to spare them the stress of restructuring the company if my health took a turn for the worse or I died unexpectedly. I had several responsibilities that I had never trained anyone to take over in my absence. There was no one who particularly wanted my position of leadership in the company either. Someone needed to be trained and prepared to step up and assume my position if something were to happen to me. I knew it would be foolish of me to try and wait to find out who that might be until my health declined even further.

After that rather scary day in the hospital, my partners and I had several meetings on the subject. No matter how hard I tried, I couldn't get them to take me seriously. They were confused and told me that I was probably just overreacting out of fear. Each of them made it painfully clear that they didn't want to assume my position of leadership. They were so concerned that they even asked my superiors from our broker dealer's office to talk me into staying for two or three more years. I had a strong sense that I wouldn't be around much longer. After trying to convince everyone several times, I was overwhelmingly frustrated. I got down on my knees and begged God to give me some clearer answers. Why was I feeling such a strong urge to plan my exit from my own business? How could I make everyone understand what I was feeling? How much time did I have left to plan my exit?

As I prayed I clearly heard the voice of God say, "March 1, 2012." Thinking that very odd, I continued to pray, hoping to get more than just a date of some unknown event. Was that the day I needed to retire? Or might it be the day I would die? Neither of my questions received an answer. Still, I knew there was something significant that would occur on that date. I felt sure my partners needed to be ready for my absence by that time. The next day I had another meeting with my leadership team. I expressed my conviction that they needed to plan to run the company without me by March 1, 2012, only nine months away. They all gave me a look of utter shock and confusion, and were curious about why I chose that particular date. It appeared I must be crazy for planning to be gone that soon with no reasonable explanation besides a strong calling from God.

I told them I had no idea why, but I strongly believed it was imperative that they be ready by that date. Over the years I had learned to trust the instincts that God had given me. I wasn't about to start doubting His plan when it concerned the well-being of so many friends and loved ones. If I was really going to die, I wanted them to be capable of continuing on with the same courage and conviction I tried to lead them with.

> **Over the years, I have learned to listen to the still small voice of God. He always directs. It's up to me to listen and obey.**

After discussing my symptoms with my personal physician again he did a series of blood tests to figure out what might be wrong. Everything came back normal. In frustration, I returned to my cardiologist and complained, "Doc, I am not a hypochondriac. Something is wrong with me. I feel like I could die any minute." He responded that he believed my problem was stemming from my cholesterol medication. He suggested that I stop taking the medication and see what happened.

After only three days off the medicine, I felt like a new man. I was certainly happy about feeling better, but still struggling to process everything that happened in my life during the previous 30 days. I had a deep sense that my strange near death experiences and my off the wall urges to retire were connected. There was a bigger picture I wasn't yet able to see. The thought of so many changes scared me. I knew that if I didn't continue to trust God, I might miss out on an important message from Him, which could cost my co-workers and loved ones dearly. Although not fully convinced that my health issues were resolved, I was confident that God was seriously up to something life altering.

Roxanne had another Haiti training session at Buddy and Casey's church the last Sunday of the month. The grandkids and I decided to go back to Billy Sims for dinner. We drove through the mile-wide swath of devastation on Rangeline Road. From the center of the damage, there was nothing but rubble as far as we could see. It took three minutes and 37 seconds to drive from the center of the destruction to the light on 7th Street. I shuddered to think what might have happened if I had turned right that night. Again, I was reminded of how God spared us. I honestly wondered why. Only halfway through 2011, and past a few brushes with death, I was sure of only two things: change was in the air and God had my full attention.

POINTS2PONDER
LIFE'S wake up call

1: How does change or the thought of change make you feel?

_____

_____

_____

_____

2: Describe a life event or experience God used to get your attention:

_____

_____

_____

_____

3: What changes did you make as a result of God's wake up call? Did the changes last? Why or why not?

_____

_____

_____

_____

4: Have you ever had a moment where you thought you might die? How did that experience change your life?

_____

_____

10 »»

caution to the
WIND

"To be heroic is to be courageous enough to die for something; to be inspirational is to be crazy enough to live a little."

- Criss Jami, *Venus In Arms*

Entering the latter half of 2011, I continued to mentally disconnect from my business. The concerns that plagued my mind in the first half of the year slowly morphed and manifested as an urgency to live every moment to its fullest without holding back. All the questions still lingering in my mind had left me in a weird funk. I tried to be very open with Roxanne about how I was feeling. I wanted her to be aware of what was going on and get her input. The crazy part was her persistent response of, "I'm not concerned about what you're feeling or what you're doing. I have peace about it." Even with the uncertainties in my mind, I trusted that God was in control.

In an employee meeting just a few days later, my partners and I officially announced that I would be phasing out of the company by early March, 2012. After that meeting I told Roxanne that I had perfect peace about the decision. She simply said, "I do, too." We spent the next two hours in the hot tub reminiscing about our life together—our courtship, our wedding, our kids and grandkids, trips we had taken and most of all, how God had led us every step of the way. We agreed to continue to trust God to lead us.

Over the next two months, Roxanne and I threw caution to the wind. We jumped at every opportunity to take a trip together. Our close friends, Ray and Judi, from California, called and said, "There is a meeting in Chicago at the end of August. Why don't you sign up and join us there?" It had been quite a while since we last visited them so we decided to go. We had a blast. We took a Segway tour of the city and I managed to crash into a statue in the park. Roxanne, however, had a flawless ride and smirked at my misfortune as she handled her Segway like a pro. We went shopping, sightseeing and enjoyed several fancy dinners together.

Later, we walked the shores of Lake Michigan. I told Ray and Judi about our crazy plans to leave the company. They were intrigued as I shared about the strange peace we both had about it. Their much needed encouragement touched my heart, and we were sad when we had to say goodbye to our special long distance friends.

After being home for only a few days, we headed out for our next adventure. It began late one evening when Roxanne made an exciting discovery while checking Facebook. "Babe," she exclaimed, "Jose and Patti are going to be performing for the next couple of months on a Norwegian cruise ship sailing out of New Orleans!" Jose and Patti sang 60's music on cruise ships, and we absolutely loved them. There was a coupon offer on their Facebook page and after checking out the cruise line website, we found a last minute deal we simply couldn't pass up. Without hesitation, we made reservations and packed our bags.

We loaded the car and headed for Louisiana with full knowledge that there was a major storm coming ashore. We planned to take an extra day to get there so we could meet a new couple, Glenn and Melissa, for lunch. They are the parents of our friend, Sarah, who had stayed in our home for a few days while she attended a training conference at our church. We enjoyed getting to know her so much during her stay, and were fascinated by her stories of serving as a missionary in Afghanistan. After seeing Roxanne's Facebook post about the trip, she immediately sent Roxanne a message. "You can't go to New Orleans without meeting my parents. They live very close to the port, so you could meet them for lunch. They are very sad right now having lost both my brother and nephew in the last few months. I know you guys could be an encouragement to them." We agreed and told her we would love to meet them.

To allow ourselves plenty of time with Glenn and Melissa, we planned an overnight stop in Clinton, Mississippi. Pulling into the hotel parking lot, I noticed a restaurant next door with a strange name, The Froghead Grill. Since I had always had a slight obsession with frogs, I jokingly exclaimed, "Hey, Babe! Let's eat there for dinner!" Surprisingly, she thought that sounded like fun and off we went.

The Froghead Grill definitely lived up to its name. There were frog pictures, frog statues, frog proverbs and even some live frogs in an aquarium. It was like frog heaven. Other than the frogs on her apron, our waitress was dressed totally in black. She had several tattoos and piercings, none of which were frogs. I thought she looked a bit out of place, but I was more than ready to give my order to whoever would take it. Roxanne, on the other hand, looked right into the girl's eyes and started speaking softly to her like I'd seen her do with many strangers before. Only a few moments passed before the girl was pouring out her life story to Roxanne. Roxanne gently encouraged her and lovingly pointed her to Jesus as the answer. I have to admit that I would probably have ordered my food and never given the waitress a second thought. After all, we were on vacation. I saw an oddly dressed waitress in a restaurant with a funny name, but Roxanne saw a precious person in need. That was her special gift.

As we headed south the next morning, it was pouring rain. I had picked up a book on tape from the Bible bookstore before we left home. I popped it into the CD player. The teaching couple soon began talking about a concept they called "divine detours." The authors defined them as moments when God steps into our lives and changes our course. As we were discussing that concept Roxanne said, "I'd better call Sarah's parents and set up our lunch plans." As she pulled out her phone, she noticed a text from Norwegian Cruise Lines informing us that, due to the weather, they had to delay our sailing at least 24 hours. Reading me the text she commented, "Well, I guess we have a divine detour. We will have to stay a night in New Orleans. At least we can take our time visiting with Sarah's parents because we won't have to rush to the ship."

Roxanne called Sarah's parents to set up our lunch and explained that because of the delay, we could spend more time with them. They insisted that we spend the night in their home. We decided not to be upset about the delayed sailing. Instead, we would trust God to turn our divine detour into a blessing. As we headed to their house, we prayed that God would show us His purpose in our detour and bless our time with them.

The 24-hour delay soon turned into a 48-hour delay, so we stayed two nights with Glenn and Melissa. The extra day we stayed over was Labor Day, which they had not planned to celebrate because they were grieving two huge losses in their lives. Sadly, both their son and grandson had passed away only two months before our visit. Since we were there, they decided to have a barbecue and invite one of their pastors to join us.

As Pastor Lawrence arrived, the conversation turned to the weather in New Orleans. Glenn and Melissa relayed how their home had suffered extensive damage during Hurricane Katrina. In fact, they had lived in Baton Rouge for a year while it was being repaired. Pastor Lawrence told us that they had turned their church into temporary living quarters for mission teams coming to New Orleans to help in the rebuilding process. He told how thousands of mission teams had come, some coming multiple times, to perform all the hard, tedious work of cleaning up and rebuilding the city. He went on to say, "You didn't hear a lot about it, but if it weren't for the Christian mission teams coming, New Orleans would never have been rebuilt." Roxanne listened intently and shared some stories of her Haiti trips. It encouraged us to hear that mission teams were making a difference, not only in places like Haiti, but at home in the States as well. We had an awesome time of fellowship and sharing what God was doing in our lives.

While visiting with Pastor Lawrence, I overheard a phone conversation between Glenn and Sarah. Sarah was living at a mission training facility about four hours from New Orleans. She had no car, so she couldn't come home or even get around without bumming a ride. One of the families in Glenn's church offered to sell her an older Toyota Camry for $400. They assured Glenn that it was in very good shape and it would be very dependable for her. Glenn told Sarah he was praying for God to supply the $400 so she could purchase the car.

When I shared the conversation with Roxanne, we both felt God calling us to provide the $400. To show our appreciation, we bought a thank you card for Glenn and Melissa and put a check inside it to cover the cost of the car. Instead of being stuck in a lonely hotel room, frustrated that we weren't on the ship, God took us on a detour in which He provided us a place to stay, good food and some wonderful new friends. He also encouraged us through Pastor Lawrence and gave us the opportunity to provide the money for Sarah to buy a car. We came to New Orleans for a cruise, but we left blessed with a newfound appreciation for mission teams, new friends and some wonderful memories. We thanked God for taking what we could have viewed as a total disaster and turning it into a blessing for everyone involved.

After that incredible experience, we could have gone home perfectly satisfied. But we still had the whole cruise ahead of us. We listened to Jose and Patti for five nights, hiked the Mayan ruins and snorkeled in Cozumel. It was an awesome trip.

Shortly after we arrived home, Travis and Elise invited us over for dinner. As we visited at the table, our three granddaughters came out in matching t-shirts and lined up in a row with goofy smiles on their faces. As they stood there giggling, it took a minute for us to realize that each of their shirts had a single word monogrammed on it. As they

stood together, the message read, "Mommy-Is-Pregnant!" We were shocked since Elise's tubal reversal had been done only two months before. Apparently, even her doctor was amazed. He remarked that never in his entire career had he seen anyone get pregnant so quickly after that procedure. He projected a delivery date of April 18, 2012—Roxanne's birthday. Needless to say, Roxanne was absolutely overjoyed. I had never seen her so excited.

At that point, we had one more trip on the calendar for 2011. We arrived home from New Orleans just nine days before we were scheduled to leave for a financial business conference in Québec, Canada. While Roxanne was at home packing her bags, I was at the office sifting through my emails. I stumbled across a message from one of our vendors telling me about a meeting in Orlando, Florida, on October 6-7. My first thought was, "I want to go and take Roxanne." Thinking myself crazy, I called her and confessed, "Babe, you're going to think I'm nuts. There is a meeting in Orlando just one week after we return from Québec. I know we have been gone a lot lately, but everything in me wants us to go." She quickly responded, "Let's do it!"

Québec was a beautiful place. We met up with Ray and Judi again. We enjoyed seeing some historic sites together as we told them about all our exciting trips we had taken since the last time we saw them. We took a city tour, went to Montmorency Falls and St. Anne Cathedral. The last evening we took a romantic night time horse and carriage ride around

the city. The trip was like a second honeymoon for us.

Less than a week later, Roxanne and I boarded a plane for Orlando. While we were there, Steve Jobs, the founder of Apple, passed away. During the meeting, the guest speaker shared one of Steve's quotes from a Stanford University commencement address in June, 2005:

"Remembering that I'll be dead soon is the most important tool I have ever encountered to help me make the big choices in life. Because almost everything—the external expectations, all pride, all fear of embarrassment or failure— these things just fall away in the face of death, leaving only what is truly important. Remembering that you are going to die is the best way I know to avoid the trap of thinking you have something to lose. You are already naked. There is no reason not to follow your heart... Stay hungry. Stay foolish."

I could really relate to that quote. I didn't know if I was going to die soon, but I did know it was possible and that realization had radically shifted my priorities. It changed the way I looked at the world, how I viewed my relationships and how I chose to spend my time. Though the thought that my life could end sooner than I hoped was still scary, I was incredibly thankful for the valuable lessons I learned as I lived out every day as if it were my last.

After the meeting, we decided to stay in Orlando for a couple more days and moved to a cheaper hotel. It rained the entire time we were there, but that didn't stop us from having a great time as we walked all over Universal Studios like love crazed teenagers. I'm not sure either one of us really understood why we were feeling the way we did. We just knew we had a chance to be together, we loved each other madly, and we wanted to enjoy every moment we possibly could together. We had thrown caution to the wind, and enjoyed four amazing trips in two months. I will be forever thankful that we did.

POINTS 2 PONDER
what REALLY MATTERS?

1: What really matters to you in life?

_____

_____

_____

_____

2: Describe a time when you made a decision that didn't make sense, yet, it later proved to be the right decision:

_____

_____

_____

_____

3: Describe a time when you felt like you should do something, but chose not to and regretted it:

_____

_____

_____

_____

4: What held you back? What would you do differently if you had the opportunity for a redo?

_____

_____

_____

_____

_____

5: Describe a time when you were called to step out in faith and follow a path when you didn't know where it would lead. What did you learn from that experience?

_____

_____

_____

_____

courageous
FAITH

"Faith isn't the ability to believe long and far into the misty future. It's simply taking God at His word and then taking the next step."

- Joni Erickson Tada

Although we had thoroughly enjoyed our travels, Roxanne and I were happy to be home in time to spend Thanksgiving with our family and friends. We always looked forward to a delicious dinner and the opportunity to reflect on the blessings God had given us throughout the year. That particular Thanksgiving, we had more reasons to express our gratitude to God than we could possibly list. I thought to myself, it could never get any better than this. I was wrong again.

Travis and Elise had planned to keep the gender of their unborn child a secret in order to tell the whole family during our Thanksgiving festivities. Because Roxanne had no biological grandchildren, she was especially eager to know if the baby would be a girl or boy. She timidly asked Elise if she could accompany her to the ultrasound appointment, promising not to breathe a word of it to anyone including me. Thankfully, Elise agreed and Roxanne was able to go. She kept that secret so that Travis and Elise could be the ones to share the news.

As soon as everyone arrived at our house for Thanksgiving, we gathered in a circle to pray for our meal. Travis and Elise's oldest daughter, Audrey, stepped into the center of our prayer circle and proclaimed, "I have an announcement to make." All eyes were on Audrey as she opened an envelope and pulled out a white card. She read aloud, "It's a girl and her name will be Chrysalyn." Roxanne's smile lit up her face like a Christmas tree. The rest of the evening was spent celebrating the wonderful news and decorating our family Christmas tree, which is one of our favorite family traditions. We told stories, took pictures, played games and pigged out on my famous turkey burritos. We'll never forget the memory of that special Thanksgiving.

When the festivities were over, it was time to go back to work. November 29, 2011, began like most mornings as I woke up early to have my quiet time and write in my journal. At the top of the journal page that morning there was an interesting quote:

"If you lose money you lose much,
If you lose friends you lose more.
If you lose faith, you lose all."
—Eleanor Roosevelt

Next to that quote I wrote this question, "What is faith, God?" I pondered for a moment before answering, "Faith is trusting God when everything seems to be out of control, yet knowing and believing deep inside that He is truly in control." Looking back on the string of out-of-character decisions I had made during the previous year, there were many things that seemed out of control, yet I was amazed at the divine peace that still flooded my heart. After my time with the Lord, I woke Roxanne. We read from our couple's devotion book and prayed together. I asked Roxanne to pray about a meeting that my partners and I would have that day concerning my future exit from the business.

As I left the business meeting at the office later that morning, I was pleased that my two partners were finally seriously considering the plan for my exit. Upon returning to my desk, I did what I do every morning; I checked my e-mails and, as always, read the "Daily Workplace Inspiration" by Os Hillman. His messages were often stirring, but that morning's devotional stopped me in my tracks. It was called, "A Heavenly Strategic Planning Session" and ended with the following paragraph:

Would you be willing to sit in the strategic planning session for your life and agree with the plans God has for your life? Could you give God complete freedom to implement that plan, no matter the cost? Ask God to give you the grace and trust in His love for you to say, "Yes."

Chills ran up and down my spine as I contemplated the gravity of that question. I found it so compelling that I copied the devotion and shared it with Roxanne the next morning. In fact, we talked about it for the next three days. We discussed how frightening it was to think about saying, "Yes," but we both had the distinct impression that God was calling us to answer the question. On the morning of December 2, 2011, during our devotion time together, we prayed and agreed, "Yes, Lord. We will say, 'Yes' to your plan even if we don't like it."

Three days later we were scheduled to host a Bible study group that we had joined a few months before. We didn't go to church that morning because Roxanne had a cold and was coughing pretty badly, but we decided to proceed with the meeting at our home that evening. Seven couples attended and I was in charge of the lesson. I printed copies of the Os Hillman devotion that had consumed my thoughts since I first read it. I told the group how Roxanne and I had wrestled with the question before we concluded that we needed to say, "Yes." I urged each couple to go home and pray together about what God would have them to do with the question.

Before our guests left, I also shared that my grandson, Jon, and I had gone to see the movie, *Courageous*, earlier that day. The movie plot involved a police officer whose 8-year-old daughter was killed in a car accident. After the accident, he had to choose whether he would be angry with God for his loss or whether he would use the tragedy as a platform to inspire others to rise up and be godly fathers. The movie concluded with the main character giving a speech at his local church where he challenged all the men in the congregation to stand up for Christ no matter what the cost. The men in that church stood one by one, pledging to be men of courage. Captivated by the scene, I wondered if I would be able to stand as well. I knew in my heart that I wanted to be a man of courage, yet, I struggled to believe that I was capable of that level of commitment.

The movie literally left me speechless for almost half an hour. All I could do was cry as I searched deep within, trying to determine how I could become that kind of man. I knew that I could easily say that I wanted to be a man of God, but I wondered how I would react if I faced a debilitating loss like the character in the movie. Would I lose hope? Would I be able to trust in God's faithfulness, knowing that He has a plan to work all things for good? I had definitely experienced the mercy and grace of God in the past as He had taken various hurts, failures and losses and turned each of those tragedies into a precious gift to me. I encouraged our group to go see the movie and contemplate its message as they considered the challenge of the devotion.

When I met with my business leadership team the following Tuesday morning, I handed them copies of the same devotion and prompted them to consider the last paragraph. I confronted them with the question, "Will you say, 'Yes' to God's plan for your personal life as well as for our business, even if you don't like it?"

After posing that thought provoking question to nearly everyone in my life, I received some tragic news that I certainly didn't like. Barb Maples, a longtime friend and client, called to tell me that her husband had passed away due to a massive heart attack the night before. I wondered how I would have responded if she had been in my Bible study group the previous Sunday and asked me to help her grasp the purpose in Don's passing. As I tried to find some words of comfort for her, I knew that nothing I could say would alleviate the grief she was experiencing.

In spite of her utter shock and broken heart, it was obvious that she was experiencing that peace of God that surpasses all understanding. In the midst of her sorrow, Barb praised God for the life He had given her with Don. Roxanne and I had attended their wedding just four short years earlier and had the privilege of seeing how happy they were together. Their relationship reminded me a lot of Roxanne and mine. I was blown away by Barb's fearlessness in the midst of such tragedy and I asked myself how I would react if I were in her shoes. If Roxanne were to pass away suddenly, would I be able to praise God and look for His purpose in it? If I were to pass away would she have that kind of courage as well? I hoped so.

When I broke the heartrending news to Roxanne, she confessed, "Babe, I can't even imagine what my life would be like if something happened to you. I don't know if I could go on without you." I assured her that I felt the same way. I mulled over that possibility the following morning as I wrote in my journal:

12-7-2011: *Lord, I want to be in the center of Your will and I am willing to do whatever it takes to get there. I probably don't have enough savings to retire, yet, I have thought about doing it anyway. My heart breaks when I think about Barb Maples, who just lost her husband. I think that if they had known what was ahead, they would have done a lot of things differently. Roxanne has been sick for a couple of weeks. The doctor gave her different antibiotics and told her to rest. I pray she will get better soon.*

I went to Don Maples' visitation alone on Thursday evening because Roxanne was still too sick to go. The next morning I went to his funeral, but promised Roxanne that I would be home in time to take her to her doctor's appointment. The funeral was a sweet celebration of Don's life and a clear picture of God's grace, which proved sufficient even in the face of death. Barb handled the occasion with incredible poise, thanking the Lord for her "four-year fairytale life" with Don. I was astonished at her sweet spirit and willingness to accept God's plan for her, even though that included losing the love of her life.

I headed home after the funeral to take Roxanne to her appointment. The doctor ordered an x-ray and said that she probably had double pneumonia. Prescribing an additional antibiotic, he told me that I should take her to the emergency room if her condition was not improved by noon the next day.

By noon the next day it was obvious that she was not getting better. In fact, she was worse, so I took her to the emergency room. The doctor on duty ordered x-rays and several blood tests. After reviewing the results he told me, "Your wife is a very sick lady. We need to admit her and get antibiotics going in an IV. She does have double pneumonia, but I'm a little concerned that pneumonia is not the primary issue.

We will run some tests to find out." As I waited for a clear answer on what was ailing Roxanne, I reflected on the events of the last eleven days. Little did I know, our lives had just taken another divine detour and God was about to test our courage and commitment to His plan in a big way.

POINTS2PONDER

CHOOSING faith over fear ▸ ≫

1: What is your greatest fear and why?

_____

_____

_____

_____

2: What does faith mean to you?

_____

_____

_____

_____

3: Describe a time when life seemed out of control and yet the outcome was surprisingly positive:

_____

_____

_____

_____

4: Describe a time when you were able to work through your fears and respond in faith. What did you learn from that experience?

_____

_____

_____

_____

_____

_____

5: When you are afraid, how do you typically react?

_____

_____

_____

_____

6: When you make a decision to trust God for the outcome, how does it make you feel?

_____

_____

_____

_____

7: God always asks us to say, "Yes" to His plan, and many times He doesn't supply the details. Instead He asks us to trust Him. Are you willing to step out in faith even if you don't like it? How would saying, "Yes" be incorporated into your daily walk with God?

_____

_____

_____

_____

dancing in the

RAIN

"My friends, love is better than anger. Hope is better than fear. Optimism is better than despair. So let us be loving, hopeful and optimistic. And we'll change the world."

- Jack Layton

was pretty clueless the first few days that Roxanne was hospitalized, thinking that she would only be there for a short time and then life would get back to normal. The following journal entries are what I wrote during that time and are a vivid snapshot of my mental and spiritual reactions to the plan that God was unfolding for us.

12–11–11: *After five hours in the ER yesterday, they moved Roxanne to ICU. She's on oxygen and some heavy duty IV antibiotics. The doctor said it was a good thing we brought her in when we did. If we had waited one more day she might have been in septic shock. Tiffany is running a half marathon today. Roxanne wants me to film her crossing the finish line so she can share the moment from her hospital room.*

12-12-11: *Roxanne is definitely feeling better this morning. The antibiotics seem to be hitting her infection. They are doing a lot of blood tests to rule out any other problems.*

12-13-11: *Roxanne seems to be feeling better. They moved her from ICU to a regular room last night. I wonder if this will affect her Haiti trip in January. She did not eat much today. She said she was craving yellow curry, so I got her some. Lord, I'm wondering what You have for us now. The business deal is sort of up in the air. I told my partners I might be leaving March 1, 2012, but now I am really not sure where we go from here. Direct our steps, our thinking and our plans. I'm trying to understand where You're leading, Lord. Please show me.*

12-14-11: *Roxanne is not feeling well this morning. They did an ultrasound on her stomach and discovered that her spleen is two to three times the normal size. Her white blood count is still way up and she still needs oxygen to breathe. They are looking for other possible problems. Lord, I pray she will begin to get better, her spleen will shrink, her white count will reduce and her breathing will normalize. I'm staying with her today because I can tell she's a bit anxious.*

That evening the doctor came in and told us that he

was convinced that Roxanne had some sort of immune deficiency. Having no idea what that meant, we asked him to explain. He replied that it could be lymphoma, leukemia, or a mass of some kind. He ordered additional tests and a bone marrow biopsy to make an accurate diagnosis.

In that moment, my heart sank and I lost all hope of going back home in a few days. It was suddenly clear that we were facing a much bigger hurdle than either of us initially thought. Tears welled up in Roxanne's eyes. I lowered her bed rails, crawled in beside her and wrapped my arms around her as much as I could. As we talked through our fears and concerns, I noticed a book sitting on Roxanne's food tray.

Out of curiosity, I picked it up and asked Roxanne where she got it. She replied that my sister, Debi, had brought it earlier that day. The book titled, *Learning to Dance in the Rain*, was based on the quote, **"Life is not about waiting for the storms to pass. It is about learning to dance in the rain."** I thought to myself, what perfect timing. Just moments after the doctors issued a terrifying report, God had sent us a powerful tool of encouragement and comfort.

Since we were both in serious need of comfort, I decided to read several short stories from the book to Roxanne. Each story and quote challenged us to look for the bright side of every situation and the silver lining to every storm cloud. We realized that there were really only two choices we could make. Option one was that we could choose to be sad, fearful and angry with God for allowing Roxanne to be sick. That would mean turning our backs on our faith and the principles we had worked so hard to teach our children. Option two was that we could continue to have faith and hope against hope, believing that somehow God would be glorified through it all no matter the cost. After reading those inspiring stories, we made a serious commitment to refuse to focus on the storm. Instead, we would "dance in the rain." We promised to remind each other of that commitment no matter how difficult or overwhelming the storm might become. I sat alone in her room that night after she dozed off, trying not to give into the discouragement that threatened to overwhelm me.

I picked up my Bible, desperately hoping that God would speak a word of encouragement to me. As I opened it, the first passage that caught my eye was Psalm 62:5-6, "Find rest, oh my soul, in God alone; my hope comes from Him. He alone is my rock and my salvation; He is my fortress, I will not be shaken." That verse gave me assurance that God would be there with us through the storm, even in the midst of all the uncertainty. I was troubled and concerned about what lay before us, but was absolutely confident that God would never leave us or forsake us.

Early the next morning, three oncologists came in and informed us that Roxanne had leukemia. They believed that it was probably a "garden variety" called Chronic Lymphocytic Leukemia or CLL, which is very treatable. They would know for sure in a couple of days. They said she could possibly start treatment from home soon. I could hardly believe it. I had spent the past several months wondering if God was warning me of my own impending death, yet, there I was with Roxanne in the hospital and she was the one who had a life threatening illness. My own health concerns evaporated as my concerns for her grew. I held her hand, trying to comfort her. My chest tightened and my heart was heavy. The moment God had spent nearly a year preparing me for had finally arrived. I realized that the strange concerns I had in the months previous had been valid, but the resulting circumstance was far different from what I had anticipated.

I cringed to think of how different those few moments would have been if I had not just spent several months facing my own fears and answering the testing questions God laid on my heart. Would I trust Him? Would I praise Him even when my hopes and dreams seemed to be crumbling before my eyes? I suddenly understood why He had asked me those same daunting questions in advance. When you have already made a choice on how to respond to those questions, it is far easier to deal with what comes your way. Both Roxanne and I had already answered, "Yes" to those questions, but deep down I knew the most important test of all was continuing to say, "Yes" even as my heart was breaking for her and also for myself at the possibility of losing her.

Roxanne tried to calm my fears as we talked the situation through. She never complained, questioned God or had a "poor me" attitude. Instead, she responded to the news with incredible grace. She was more concerned with caring for me and making sure the kids were okay than she was about herself. In her gentle way she reminded me that God was in control and her trust would remain in Him. She made it clear that she was going to continue saying, "Yes" to God's plan.

Her loving response gave me the courage to say, "Yes" again as well. A new part of our journey had begun and we prayed together that we would have the strength and wisdom to continue to follow the Lord's plan for us daily. We both had peace after that prayer. After talking it over, Roxanne and I agreed that we needed to tell the kids about the diagnosis as soon as possible. Fighting back tears, I called each one and explained that we had some news and a family meeting was set for seven o'clock that evening. I dreaded the thought of how everyone would react, especially since I was in shock and didn't know how to react myself. My future seemed to be disappearing into a haze and I was speechless. Despite how God prepared us both for a drastic life event, it was still difficult to grasp the reality that the love of my life was dangerously ill. I hoped and prayed that God would give us all the grace to accept the news that Roxanne had cancer and choose not to be angry with Him. My biggest fear was that I might fall apart before I could get the news across, or that I might not be strong enough to support them fully because of my own emotional turmoil.

When they arrived, I could tell that they were worried. They gathered in a circle around Roxanne's bed as I explained the diagnosis. Tears streamed down their faces as we each prayed for healing. When we finished, the room was heavy with silence. They each hugged her as they left and she did her best to encourage them and to keep their spirits up. When everyone left I crawled up into the hospital bed with Roxanne. As we cried together, each moment seemed like hours.

12-18-11: *What a week, Lord. We thought we might get to go home yesterday, but she still has too much fluid on her lungs.*

We made a 50-yard walk up and down the hall. That was a victory. Three different people came to pray for Roxanne and all three of them told me they believed God was going to heal her. I know You can heal her completely, God. I just don't know if that's Your plan. If it is, I praise You. If You'd like, You can speak it to me and I will stand on it. But I know that You don't heal everybody, Lord. That is not always Your plan. God, I want to hear You. I want to be sensitive to Your spirit. Speak, Lord. I am listening.

"Team Roxanne" was established that same day. I started sending text message updates to about 30 people, but that number quickly grew to 80. I later learned that many of those people were forwarding the texts to a list of their own. In the beginning, I simply gave health updates and specific prayer requests. Before long, Team Roxanne became our special prayer team. I began to share our journey, both emotionally and spiritually. Later, I received testimonies from several people who received Team Roxanne texts on a specific day, which consequently helped them get through issues in their own lives. Hearing those testimonies was a huge encouragement to us both. I hoped that by openly conveying my fears, anxieties and hopes that others would see that joy in Christ is possible even in the worst moments of life. That definitely proved to be true for us. Like the journal entries, the texts to Team Roxanne give a first hand glimpse into what I was feeling and what God taught me along the way.

Text to Team Roxanne **December 18, 2011:** *Yesterday was a good day. I am amazed at how the definition of a "good day" can change so quickly. A 50-yard walk down the hospital corridor becomes an amazing victory. An extra moment in a hug sends a message unspoken, but felt in a comforting and empowering way. Experiencing God's peace in a moment that it does not make sense is the greatest proof that He is Lord.*

The next day began early with a bone marrow biopsy. The anesthesia sent Roxanne into respiratory distress. As our hospitalist, Dr. Webb, attempted to stabilize her breathing, I asked her why Roxanne seemed to be struggling to breathe. She responded that Roxanne had a type of leukemia that produces fluid. The fluid was accumulating in her lungs, resulting in labored breathing. I asked if she knew what type of leukemia Roxanne had. She replied that it was called T-cell Prolymphocytic Leukemia or TPLL.

Once I knew that Roxanne was settled back into her room, I slipped down to the waiting area and searched the internet for further information on TPLL. The description was grim. TPLL is a very rare, extremely aggressive form of leukemia, which is very difficult to treat. The average life expectancy of someone diagnosed with TPLL is only 7.5 months. Only one drug had been fairly successful in putting it into remission, but the only hope of a cure was a bone marrow transplant. Without a transplant, the disease would come roaring back out of remission.

I then had the first of many moments in which all I could do was put my hands over my eyes and sob uncontrollably. I determined not to tell anyone what I knew until Dr. Schnider, our oncologist, confirmed the diagnosis himself. He finally arrived and vaguely reported, "It's not CLL. It's a different form of leukemia called TPLL. It calls for a different type of treatment, which we will be starting soon." I followed him out into the hall and confronted him with what I had read. He confirmed that it was an aggressive form of leukemia that is difficult to treat, but he assured me that they would be doing everything they could do to beat it.

When I went back into the room, Roxanne said, "Babe, I didn't understand a thing he just said." I felt an enormous weight settle on me because of what I had read about TPLL earlier that morning. I knew I had to protect her from discouragement as much as I could and I couldn't bear to tell her how grim the prognosis really was. I decided not to burden her with details that might make the situation even more difficult for her to handle and simply said, "Babe, in a nutshell, it is worse than we thought and it's a bigger hurdle than we thought. But remember, we promised that we are not going to focus on the storm. Rather, we are going to 'dance in the rain.'"

Bobby and my niece, Tahnee, were in the room with us. As we prayed, it was as if God dropped a warm blanket of peace down from heaven and wrapped all four of us in it. It was a peace like

I had never known before. Afterwards, each one of us shared how we had experienced the same cloak of comfort. We all left awestruck that we could feel so calm in such a solemn moment.

12-20-11: *Roxanne had lots of visitors today. I spent the day talking to doctors about whether we should move her to MD Anderson or some other cancer research hospital. I think they took me seriously about moving her, but Dr. Schnider thinks we need to start treatment right away and then start looking for a place to move her. He said we needed to do a hospital-to-hospital transfer because she was too sick to be released. They pulled 1.5 liters of fluid off her right lung today. Travis and Elise came by and told us that they decided on a middle name for their baby girl. Her name is going to be Chrysalyn Roxanne. Needless to say, Roxanne was elated. She told Travis, "That's just all the more reason for me to fight."*

12-21-11: *I went home late last night to try to get a little sleep. I woke up at 3:30 AM feeling like I needed to go to the hospital. When I got there Roxanne had been struggling with her oxygen level and was really anxious. I decided that I wouldn't leave her alone again. God, I'm praying for successful treatment, successful bone marrow transplant, and a full recovery in Jesus' name.*

At that moment, I didn't realize that the decision to never leave Roxanne alone again was probably the most significant decision I had ever made in my life. Until then, nearly everything in my life was scheduled around my business appointments and responsibilities, but from that point forward nothing mattered except Roxanne. All the energy I had been spending to further my career was redirected into keeping her comfortable and helping her get well again.

Dr. Schnider came in early the next morning and said, "We can do a hospital-to-hospital transfer to either UAMS in Little Rock or Barnes Jewish Hospital in St. Louis. If you want me to do that, I will facilitate the transfer. My concern is that it will take a week for them to do their testing and start treatment. In light of that fact, I think we should start treatment today and wait to decide where to transfer. I believe the sooner we start treatment, the better her chances are." We told him that we trusted his decision and were in favor of starting treatment immediately.

Two hours later Dr. Schnider called me on my cell phone saying, "The fluid they pulled from her lungs yesterday contained cancer cells. Due to that development, I think we should send her to UAMS immediately. They have agreed to take her and they have a dedicated leukemia unit and the capability to do the bone morrow transplant there. They have also committed to start treatment as soon as possible."

As the nurses prepared Roxanne for the transfer, she asked me to have Travis, Elise, Bobby, Tiffany and Jon come to visit with her one at a time. She had a steady stream of visitors all day, but she insisted on speaking with each of our children individually before she left for Little Rock. Each of them shared with me what she said to them in that meeting. They all had a very similar experience. As they came in the room, she gave them a big hug and said, "I love you very much. I'm planning to beat this. I'm going to fight it and I fully expect to make it. But, in case I don't, there are some things I want to tell you. No matter what happens, do not be mad at God. I have full faith and trust in God's plan. Roger will be there for you. He will love you and be dad to you. He might need someone, so don't be upset if he remarries. I would want him to. Live your life for God. Choose a godly spouse. Raise godly children and read them Bible stories every night. I'm very proud of you."

I saw the relief on Roxanne's face after she spoke to each of them. I was amazed at her commitment and courage to share her heart. None of us fully understood why it was so important to her to say those things at the time. Since then I have seen what a gift it was to them. It serves as a constant reminder to keep their eyes on the Lord rather than the circumstance at hand.

POINTS2PONDER

Storm dancing in life's mosh pit ▶ ▶

1: How do you normally react to bad news?

_____

_____

_____

_____

2: What do you think it means to not focus on the storm, but to dance in the rain?

_____

_____

_____

_____

3: Why do you think it was so important for Roxanne to share what she did with each of her children?

_____

_____

_____

_____

4: If you had been one of her children, how do you think her words would have affected you?

_____

_____

_____

_____

_____

_____

5: If you were facing a serious illness, what things would you want to say to each of your loved ones or your children?

_____

_____

_____

_____

christmas in
LITTLE
ROCK

"There's always going to be bad stuff out there. But here's the amazing thing... light trumps darkness every time. You can stick a candle into the dark, but you can't stick the dark into the candle."

- Jodi Picoult

oxanne's nurses spent several hours preparing her for the transfer to Little Rock. They shuffled in and out as we waited for the ambulance to arrive. Family and friends poured into Roxanne's hospital room to wish her well and say goodbye. Though exhausted, she did her best to smile, visit with and appreciate each person for coming. Finally, I asked everyone to go home and let her rest for the long night ahead.

Roxanne was very concerned about the three-hour ambulance ride. We both knew it was going to be tough. When the ambulance arrived, the crew wouldn't let me ride with her and warned me not to try to keep up with them. I was devastated at the thought of her having to go alone. I kissed her goodbye, my tears dripping onto her face. She assured me, "I'm going to be just fine, Babe. I'll see you in Little Rock."

Roxanne's dear friend, Tina, was the last to leave the hospital. She volunteered to gather up our belongings and distribute all the flowers and plants to other patients as Roxanne had requested. It amazed me that despite her weakened condition, Roxanne was still thinking of the well being of others. I was more proud of her loving and kind spirit at that moment than I ever had been. I hugged and thanked Tina, then jogged to my car secretly hoping I could keep up with the ambulance.

About an hour into the trip, Roxanne sent me a text saying, "Babe, I'm doing great. God is with me." Overwhelmed with emotion, I struggled to see the road through my tears. For a guy who had shed very few tears in his life, I was really making up for lost time. Unfortunately, I never even saw the ambulance and they beat me to Little Rock by 45 minutes.

It was midnight when I finally found a place to park and someone who could direct me to Roxanne's room. Over the next three hours we saw a steady stream of doctors, nurses and lab technicians. We finally went to sleep about 3:00 AM, only three days before Christmas. We hadn't slept long before an unbelievably busy day began. She had eight diagnostic procedures, including a bone marrow biopsy. At the end of the day, after the installation of a tube in her right side to drain the fluid from her lung, she was absolutely exhausted. She even slept through the arrival of her sisters, Wanda and Nelli. They had driven all the way from Virginia to visit her.

Roxanne woke up later that night in tremendous pain from the incision in her side. We called for pain medicine, but the nurse never came. I had to get pretty firm before someone finally took care of her. Fortunately, that was the only nurse we had any problems with in our entire hospital experience. That one negative incident made us even more appreciative of all the other great nurses we had.

The next morning, a wonderful nurse named Diane, explained that Roxanne would have a day of rest while all the tests from the day before were being processed. Roxanne's sisters arrived at the hospital early, anxious to visit with her. They had barely settled in when Sandra Hedrick, a business friend, arrived with her siblings and her children to sing Christmas carols for us. The amazing performance ministered to all of us and brought tears to our eyes. When they finished singing, I opened the door to find all the nurses gathered outside listening.

The head of the oncology department came by that evening to inform us that they had confirmed the diagnosis of TPLL and would be starting treatment in the next 24 hours. The plan was to start with a small dose of the chemotherapeutic agent to see how Roxanne would tolerate it, then increase the dosage over a three-day period. There would be three chemo treatments each week. She went on to say that if Roxanne continued to respond well, we might be able to go home and receive the treatments at the oncology center in Rogers, Arkansas.

Text to team Roxanne **December 23, 2011:**   *The head of the oncology department came in and said they are going to start treatments in the next 24 hours. She explained all the risks and possible side effects. Since this is the only drug that has been effective in her type of leukemia, please pray that:*

1. Roxanne can tolerate the drug with minimal complications or side effects.
2. The drug will successfully put the leukemia into remission.
3. The right donor will surface and a successful bone marrow transplant will provide a cure.
4. We will go through this whole experience in a way that honors and glorifies God.
5. God does a miracle. Our Hope is in Him.

After a difficult night of struggling to breathe, Roxanne awoke feeling a little better on Christmas Eve morning. Knowing that her mom, dad, three sisters, brother-in-law and nephew were on their way from Missouri, Roxanne asked the nurse if she could have a bath so she could wash and comb her hair. The nurse answered, "A sponge bath—yes, but washing your hair is just not possible."

From the beginning Roxanne had been a remarkable patient, always smiling and kind to the nurses and staff although they sometimes inflicted pain in the process of caring for her. She tried hard to remain upbeat even when receiving bad news, but when the nurse said she couldn't wash her hair, she began to cry. "My family and my kids are all coming for Christmas," she said through her tears. "Isn't there some way we can wash my hair?" He was trying to be firm, but his face softened at the sight of her tears and he finally answered, "I'll see what I can do."

Within a few minutes, an LPN named Tony, walked in and announced, "If your husband will help me, we will get your hair washed for you right there in your bed." Roxanne's face lit up at the news. Tony got a bucket of water, and gave me a big trash bag to catch the water in. In minutes we managed to get the job done. Another nurse gently gave her a sponge bath, rubbed lotion on her body and helped Roxanne comb and fix her hair. I will never forget the look of gratitude on Roxanne's face as they got her cleaned up. That experience was yet another reminder of what a unique ministry nursing really is.

Roxanne looked beautiful when her family arrived and we all had a great visit. The head of the oncology department came by to tell us that the first treatment would begin at 10 PM. After her family left, Roxanne and I talked about the journey we were on and our commitment to "dance in the rain" no matter the cost. I assured her that I would be right by her side through thick and thin and that I would love and take care of the kids. I held her close as we both softly cried. Later that evening, as Roxanne slept, I wrote in my journal.

12-24-2011-10 PM: *Well, Lord, in 14 short days my life has been turned upside down. Only two weeks ago I thought my wife had the flu. We went from a diagnosis of flu to double pneumonia, to CLL (a type of leukemia that is very treatable), to TPLL (a very rare and aggressive leukemia). I went from having an incredible life and marriage to having a wife with a life-threatening disease. It's unbelievable how fast life can change. On December 2, I said, "YES" I would agree to Your plan for my life, even if I don't like it. So far, Lord, I don't like it. Yet, You have given me "peace that passes all understanding." Even still— wow, Lord! A lady just came in, hung a big bag of chemo on the IV pole and left the room. It's the first treatment, a smaller amount to see how Roxanne will react. It's so scary. To top it all off, the nurse didn't say one word to me. I could lose her, Lord. I could lose the love of my life. I don't want to and I hope that is not Your plan. Still, my hope and trust is in You.*

Hearing my prayer and knowing that I needed support, Tony, the LPN, walked back in and sat down beside me. He shared a verse of scripture and encouraged me. We talked for a while before he prayed for us. As he said goodbye, I was strengthened and revived by his visit. God is always right on time.

Tony had not been gone long when Roxanne woke up saying she was cold. I put another blanket on her, but she began to shake violently. Just as I pressed the call button, she began to vomit. The tremors went on for several minutes before the nurse gave her an injection, which helped her to relax. It was terrifying. I wanted to scream, "Stop! Unhook her!" Yet, I realized that our only real hope, short of a miracle, was to walk through the pain of chemo in order to rid her body of cancer. When she finally relaxed enough to go back to sleep, I prayed desperately for her to have the fortitude to endure future chemo treatments and that she would have enough strength to enjoy Christmas with the family the next day.

Roxanne was tired when she awoke on Christmas morning. The shaking spell from the previous night made her anxious about the next treatment, but she was also very excited that all our kids and grandkids were on their way to Little Rock. Tiffany and Bobby arrived first with a small Christmas tree, lights, ornaments and decorations. Roxanne watched with a little smile on her face as Tiffany decorated the room and Bobby brought in all the gifts from our home. As he placed them around the little Christmas tree, I could see the sparkle in Roxanne's eyes as she realized that we were not going to miss Christmas after all.

Next came Travis, Elise and the three girls, with Jon following right behind them. They added their gifts to the pile that Bobby had made. Casey called to let us know they were still a few hours away. Since the room was full already, we decided to go ahead and do Christmas with our immediate family. The next few hours were the most precious hours I've ever lived. We had Roxanne

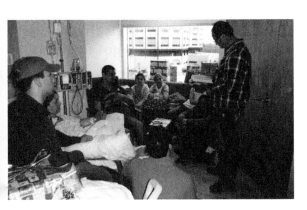

sitting up in a chair with Bobby on one side and Jon on the other, each holding her hand. It was a time of laughter and tears. I read the Christmas story and we exchanged gifts. I can't recall any of the gifts, but I do remember the overwhelming spirit of love and oneness. We were all tremendously thankful for the chance to be together, even if it was in a small and uncomfortable hospital room.

We didn't ask permission to have our little celebration, we just did it and the nurses were kind enough to leave us alone. As we were wrapping up, my cell phone rang and Casey told me that the lady at the front desk said no children were allowed on Roxanne's floor, much less in her room. I slipped out and spoke to the nearby charge nurse. "My daughter and her children drove six hours to spend Christmas with their Grandma. I will bring them straight to the room and they will not leave the room until we are done. I promise that we'll be very quiet." She looked me straight in the eye and said, "We will probably be too busy to notice that you let them in. Just be sure they are gone by 7 PM when the night shift comes on." I don't know if you're supposed to hug the charge nurse, but I sure did.

There wasn't a nurse in sight when I opened the security door for Casey and the kids. It was as if they had cleared the halls for "Operation Christmas" to sneak in. We spent the next two hours celebrating Jesus, our family and each other. It was truly the best Christmas I think any of us had ever experienced.

Roxanne was exhausted and needed to rest before her treatment, so all the kids and grandkids found a large waiting room filled with recliners. They put the recliners in a big circle and sat and talked. Before they left to go eat, I walked down to say goodbye and suggested we make a prayer circle and pray for Roxanne's treatment, which was coming up in a couple of hours. I asked them to pray that she would have no reactions and that everything would go smoothly.

There were six of our grandchildren in that prayer circle who were less than 12 years of age. Five of them prayed out loud for their grandmother. I couldn't have been more proud. I told the grandkids that God especially hears the prayers of children and I believed that their grandma's treatment was going to be trouble free because of their prayers. Four hours later, the treatment was over and it went exactly as we prayed.

She had no reactions and rested comfortably the whole time.

I have forgotten most of the Christmas gifts I've ever received. I don't really remember parties I've attended or even church services, but I will never forget what I learned that year. That Christmas, the best gift we all received was being together as a family and having the peace that only God can bring during what was the most difficult situation we had ever faced. That year the material gifts didn't seem to matter half as much as a hug or smile from a loved one. We learned that Christmas is not about fancy holiday food, gifts, parties, or even church services, it's about the love God has for us, and the love we have for each other. With love, every day is another gift.

1: If you knew this was your family's last Christmas together, what would you buy them?

_____

_____

_____

_____

2: What is the greatest gift you have ever received and why was it meaningful to you?

_____

_____

_____

_____

3: What changes could you make to center your holiday season more on the love of Christ and each other rather than gifts?

_____

_____

_____

_____

4: Describe a time when someone's small act of kindness had a profound effect on your life:

_____

_____

LOVE
trumps fear

"Courage is not the absence of fear, but rather the judgement that something else is more important than fear."

- Ambrose Redmoon

Having just experienced Christmas in the most unlikely of places, I needed to make a trip back home and take care of some business that was left undone when they transferred Roxanne to Little Rock. Casey agreed to stay with Roxanne, so after her third treatment I drove back to Bentonville to tie up some loose ends. I made it home, went straight to my bed and collapsed from sheer exhaustion.

The next morning I did laundry, paid a few bills and scheduled a meeting with my business partners. Struggling to focus, I constantly fought the urge to get in my truck and drive back to Roxanne. I found it nearly impossible to concentrate on anything, having severely underestimated how hard it would be to be away from her. I tried to get everything done as quickly as possible.

Roxanne called the next morning, trying to sound positive, but I could hear the anxiety in her voice. I knew that Casey wouldn't leave her alone for a second and would take good care of her, but I knew she would be most comfortable if I was there for her. I met with my partners and informed them that I might not be back until I could bring Roxanne home for good and that they were pretty much on their own. I could only hope that the events of last year had prepared them, because I had made up my mind not to leave Roxanne again. When I was confident that they were properly briefed on how to run the business in my absence, I practically ran to my truck and drove like a madman back to the hospital in Little Rock.

I breathed a sigh of relief as soon as I saw her face. I'm not sure which of us was happier, but we were definitely thrilled to be together again. I was surprised at how comfortable I felt in that hospital room where most people dread staying for any length of time. At that moment, I knew that my home was not back in Bentonville anymore. It was wherever Roxanne was.

As New Year's Day approached, things seemed to slow down for the first time since treatments had begun. To pass the time, I decided to get an early start on my personal New Year's tradition. Each year on New Year's Eve, I would read my previous year's journal and write a summary of the year. The process of re-examining my journal entries for 2011 was very enlightening.

It occurred to me that I had spent the entire year of 2011 trying to prepare my partners for my exit, yet not really understanding why. During the latter half of the year, I took Roxanne on trip after trip as if there would be no tomorrow. Several times I had wondered if God were hinting that my life was coming to an end. I had decided that if that were the case I wanted to leave Roxanne with lots of great memories.

Reading the last few pages of my 2011 journal made me wonder if the current detour we found ourselves on could be the reason for our seemingly irrational behavior throughout the year. Could that have been God's way of forewarning and preparing us for what was coming?

As I wrapped up my summary on New Year's Eve, Roxanne and I prepared to settle in for the night. Suddenly the door opened and I was shocked to see my sister, Debi. She announced, "I just decided I wanted to spend New Year's Eve with Roxanne." With that, she pulled the recliner up beside Roxanne's bed, tilted it back, took Roxanne's hand and settled in with us. We watched the TV to see the ball drop in Times Square, wished each other, "Happy New Year" and went to sleep.

The ladies had a sweet visit the next morning. Much more than sisters-in-law, they had become best friends over the years. Debi called Roxanne every morning on her way to work and they would talk for about 20 minutes. I saw the tender love in my sister's eyes as they chatted about girl stuff. I knew her heart was breaking when she said, "It's time for me to head back." She cried as I walked her to the elevator and hugged her goodbye. When I got back to the room Roxanne said, "That was so sweet. Can you believe she drove all the way here, slept in that awful recliner and held my hand all night? She is really a special friend."

I could tell by the look in Roxanne's eyes that she didn't feel well. We had another little pep talk and reminded ourselves that we would stay the course, not get discouraged by setbacks and continue to trust the Lord. She slept most of that day. Bobby dropped by for a while and later Tiffany came by. Their parting hugs told me that they were worried, so I tried to encourage them. Watching them leave, I asked God to surround them with His peace.

In my journal on **1-2-2012,** I wrote:
What have I learned from 24 days in the hospital?

1. Nursing is a special ministry.

2. Showing love and care goes a long way to soothe pain, lighten the load and give hope.

3. Indifference and lack of caring can intensify the pain and stress and create hopelessness.

4. The "peace that passes all understanding" is incredibly real and powerful. It is clearly supernatural and only comes when you really need it.

5. When you truly love someone and they are in crisis, nothing else really matters. Being there for that person trumps everything else.

6. I can sit in a hospital for 24 hours a day and be just fine.

7. Crisis has a way of demolishing all religious, denominational, racial, social and financial barriers.

8. When you feel something, share it while you still can.

9. When you don't know what to say, try this: "I'm here for you. I don't know what to say except that I care, I'm praying for you, I'm sorry you're going through this." Those things let a person know you care without trying to fix the problem. Some things can't be fixed.

10. God does not always do things the way we want, but He is still in control and His peace is still very available.

11. Medication can be a wonderful blessing.

12. Everyone needs encouragement. Give it freely. You may never know how much it helps.

Lord, I pray that the treatments will work and that she'll be able to get off the oxygen so we can go home soon and do treatments there.

The head of the oncology department came in early the next morning and told us that the treatments were not working as quickly as they had hoped. She went on to say that she had talked to some experts in St. Louis about Roxanne's case and was expecting a return call from the head of oncology there. That meant we definitely couldn't go home yet.

A strange peace swept over me. It was as if God was responding to my prayers the night before, "No, Son, we are not going to do it that way, but I am with you." As I opened my journal to record that thought, I stumbled upon a quote from Corrie Ten Boom: "If God sends us on stony paths, He provides stronger shoes." I had known for a long time that God answers our prayers in one of three ways—yes, no or wait. In that moment I realized that I was going to have to learn to accept His "no." I knew I just had to trust Him to give me strong enough shoes.

Thankfully, a couple of encouraging things happened which kept our spirits up. My Aunt Pat and Uncle Tom came to visit and pray with Roxanne. Their presence and prayers were uplifting to both of us. Roxanne also received a little gift in the mail from her friend, Judi, in California. It was an "Angel of Joy." I saw her perk up immediately as she gazed at her new trinket. It's astounding how little things can mean so much.

Early the next morning, I had to take Roxanne to the restroom because she was severely nauseated. The nurse came by and gave her an injection so she could rest and we got her back into bed. I was so drained that I sank to the floor next to her bed and cried out to my Lord. I told Him that I was weak, fearful and unable to carry this burden any longer. Then, I asked Him what I needed to do. My mind swirled with, "why's" and "what if's." Then, as I sat on the floor weeping, I got a text message from my dear friend and prayer warrior, Becky.

Becky's text was as follows:

We are powerless against this mighty army. We do not know what to do. We are looking to You for help. Do not be afraid. Don't be discouraged by this mighty army, for the battle is not yours, but God's. You will not even need to fight—stand still and watch God's victory. Believe the Lord your God and you will be able to stand firm.

(II Chronicles 20:12b, 15b, 17a)

It was as if God had spoken to me directly from heaven. Awestruck at the directness and timing of His answer, I was overwhelmed by a sense of peace and renewed strength. At that moment, I knew in my heart that I could carry on.

As the days passed, Roxanne and I perfected our hospital routine. I learned to cover her IV's and the catheter to help her take a shower each morning. I emptied and measured her fluids and tracked her medications, procedures and even her food intake. I quickly discovered that a new nurse coming on at shift change only knows what has been recorded in the medical record and what they are told from the previous shift. They often ask the patient a lot of questions, but a heavily medicated patient usually doesn't know the answer. I determined to know everything that was going on with Roxanne: the nurses and doctors caring for her, the medications, procedures, tests and every conversation that took place in her room. That focus on my part became vital over the following weeks. If not for my extensive knowledge of Roxanne's routine and allergies, she would have been given incorrect medications on several different occasions. Thankfully, I was able to prevent that and the nurses and doctors grew to trust me more than the computerized medical record.

The fluid-producing aspect of Roxanne's cancer caused her a lot of grief. My little 140 pound wife grew to more than 200 pounds in a fairly short amount of time and the gain was all fluid. The extreme swelling made it hard for her to walk, so I helped her to the restroom to protect her from falling. I regularly rubbed and massaged her legs and feet with lotion, which really seemed to help her. When she felt well enough, we would walk the hall. I never dreamed that I was capable of living in a hospital and serving as caregiver for my wife, but I counted every moment a privilege. I desperately wanted to care for her as perfectly as she had always cared for me.

The 22 days we spent in Little Rock were much like a roller coaster ride. We had good and bad days, encouraging and discouraging days and a few downright scary days. I was thankful for the times that Roxanne felt really great. God seemed to give her the strength she needed for special times when family and friends were there, allowing her to speak very clearly and wisely to them. At other times she was a very sick girl. Through it all, she was always smiling, happy, pleasant, kind and ready to encourage the nurses and the people who came to visit her. Even when she was in a great deal of pain she always tried to be upbeat and positive. Even when she was not up for a visit, she remained gracious and would say to me, "Babe, I'm really tired and weary. Please apologize for me because I need to rest."

After the shaking episode on Christmas Eve, her treatments went well with no visible side effects. She seemed to perk up and feel better for a couple of days afterward. She couldn't eat much except for right after a treatment and by then she was starving. She would always crave something specific to eat, so I'd try to find it. She had yellow curry, fajitas, jalapeno pepper sandwiches and Chick-Fil-A nuggets, just to name a few of her strangest selections. The funniest craving came at 2 AM when I awoke to her asking, "Babe, are you awake? I'm dying for a peanut butter and jelly sandwich." Fortunately, I was able to find one and she ate as if she'd been starving for days.

The doctors kept telling us we would be able to go home soon and do the treatments at the oncology center in Rogers. They would set a projected release date and then change it because they couldn't get her fluids completely drained and she still needed oxygen to breathe. After a while, Roxanne got really homesick. She started telling every doctor or nurse that came in her room, "I want to go home!" I started to wish they hadn't mentioned it, because every time they said no, I had to watch her heart break all over again. I kept trying to encourage her that we needed to trust the doctors to know when the time was right, but I could see the day coming when she would look me in the eye and say, "Babe, please take me home now."

Early one morning, after I gave Roxanne a shower and got her back in bed comfortably, I sat down to write a text to Team Roxanne and update them on the situation.

Text to Team Roxanne **January 6, 2012:** *Sitting in the dark in the hospital with the person you love with all your heart after a fairly rough night is a remarkable test of one's faith. I have now moved beyond just reporting Roxanne's condition to you. I'm sharing the journey. You might find yourself in a similar situation at any moment, so my babblings might prove helpful. I've never been here before, but I realize that everything I've done before now matters in this moment. I read a quote in my journal today by Clement of Alexandria. "If you do not hope, you will never find out what is beyond your hope." So who is my hope in? God? Absolutely! So should I pack her up, take her home and expect God to heal her? Not unless I get a direct word from God Himself instructing me to do that. Is my hope in medicine? Yes, but should I blindly trust it? No. Is my hope in Team Roxanne? Somewhat, yes. Your prayers and encouragement matter more than I have ever understood before. It is a delicate balance. It's not as simple as claiming, "by His stripes we are healed." If it were, the earth would be full of really old but healthy people. My dear friend, Barb Maples, lost her husband in his sleep a few weeks ago. He was healed completely, just not the way we would've chosen. My point is this: we can hope in medicine, each other, or for a miracle, but our true hope is in the love of Christ alone. Sometimes balancing that in life is just stinking hard. But praise God, in Him we can always have hope.*

Early Friday morning, January 13, 2012, the head of the oncology department came in and said, "We have been hoping to get you healthy enough to go home. We are waiting on some test results now. If the results look good, we may let you go today. You will do two to four months of treatments at the oncology center in Rogers. If they can get your cancer into remission, you will go to Barnes Jewish Hospital in St. Louis for a bone marrow transplant. You'll be there for three to five months. The transplant you need is a bit too complex for us here at UAMS."

The next few hours were incredibly frustrating. It was a stressful day and we nearly gave up on the idea that she might go home. Then, to our surprise and delight, a nurse came in mid-afternoon to tell us that Roxanne had been released. At that moment, we couldn't decide whether to be excited or scared to death. The frustration continued, since it took four hours to get her prescriptions filled in their pharmacy and to load all her stuff in my little Nissan truck. I knew it was going to be an intensely uncomfortable ride home for Roxanne, but she was such a trooper. She was just thrilled to be going home.

Thankfully we made the three and a half hour drive home without any serious problems. Unfortunately, by the time we got home, she was filled with fluid and pretty sick. With the help of my precious neighbor, Paula, we got her to bed. She was so happy to be home in our bed. She took my hand and held it all night.

As I sat in bed with her that night, I praised God that we were able to make it home without a serious emergency. I listened carefully to her breathing, hoping that the fluid buildup from the drive home wouldn't complicate her breathing. Anxious that we had a full weekend ahead of us before her next doctor's appointment, I prayed for the Lord to help us get through the weekend without a crisis.

The next morning, I turned my kitchen table into a makeshift pharmacy. I started a logbook on all her medications and procedures. I felt pretty confident that I could take care of her, but this was the first time in 36 days that she had been off oxygen and out of the hospital. I was thankful that I had been so involved in her care at the hospital. Otherwise, I wouldn't have had the slightest clue how to take care of her at home. It suddenly occurred to me that I was now her primary caregiver and there were no experts in the hall to lend a hand or give me advice.

I have to admit, that realization was just a little bit scary. Regardless, I knew I had a unique opportunity. While I could not take the cancer away, no matter how badly I wanted to, I could make the experience as pleasant and comfortable as possible for Roxanne. By allowing myself to leave my business behind, I was able to dedicate every waking moment to her care. I had spent most of my life trying to make a difference in the lives of people in a financial and spiritual sense. Now I counted it both a privilege and a blessing to be able to make a difference in the life of the person I loved most - my wife.

POINTS2PONDER
TRUMPING fear ▸ »

1: What do you do normally do when you don't know what else to do?

_____

_____

_____

_____

2: Is your response to the first question a healthy or unhealthy response, and why?

_____

_____

_____

_____

3: Describe a time in your life when you let fear cause you to shrink back and a loved one was hurt as a result:

_____

_____

_____

_____

4: Share a time when loved triumphed over fear in your life:

_____

_____

_____

nourishing
**YOUR
LOVE**

"Greater love has no man than this, than to lay down his life for his friends."

- John 15:13

After Roxanne's release from the hospital in Little Rock, all I could do was cry out to God for help, leaning on Him in each passing moment. At times it seemed like all the strength I had left was gone and when I began to lose hope, I felt the hand of God on my shoulder. His loving voice reminded me, "I'm here, son." He gave me peace at every point of the ride.

During the first weekend home, Roxanne was delighted with simple joys such as eating the delicious potato soup that her sister, Sandra, made and visiting with Travis, Bobby and Tiffany. I was, on the other hand, becoming increasingly alarmed by the amount of fluid building up in her body. Her abdomen was so swollen that I wondered how she could eat. She could barely walk, even with me helping her. She desperately wanted a hot bath, so I helped her into the tub, but I worried that I wouldn't be able to get her out. I decided after we got her safely back in bed that I wouldn't try that again unless someone was there to help in case of an emergency.

With the anxiety ridden weekend behind us, we prepared to head to Fayetteville for her first appointment at the oncology clinic. Her swelling was even more apparent by the fact that her clothes were too tight. Although I knew Roxanne didn't want to return to the hospital and she was afraid of being re-admitted, part of me hoped that she would be, so that her swelling could be monitored more carefully. When the doctor examined her, he was equally concerned about her distended state and gave her an additional water pill to rid her body of the excess fluid. By Wednesday he intended to have a clearer plan of action for a more aggressive treatment plan.

As I packed our stuff back into the car, Roxanne told me that she really liked her doctor and nurses. She was so glad we were able to continue to stay at home and work with them rather than be stuck back in a hospital. Despite her optimism, I was still on edge about how weak she was. She was easily winded after very little exertion and still needed my help to get around the house. That day I poured my heart out onto the pages of my journal.

1-18-12: Lord, Roxanne is so weak this morning that she can barely stand. She is eating very little and I'm thankful that we're going back to the doctor today at 10:15. I don't know if we can keep her out of the hospital or even if we should. It is getting more and more difficult for me to handle her. Lord, give the doctors wisdom. Help, Lord! I am struggling to keep my eyes off of the storm right now, but I trust You. Even still, I feel so weak. Give me strength for my unbelief. In Jesus' name, I pray for total healing. It's as simple as that. And if You're not going to heal her, please don't let her suffer, Lord.

When we returned to the oncologist's office on Wednesday, Roxanne was put on oxygen to help her labored breathing. Dr. Schnider had consulted with oncologists at Barnes Jewish Hospital in St. Louis. He recommended that we resume her chemo treatments that day and continue with the three treatments per week until remission occurred or the treatments had proven ineffective.

Much to my relief, Roxanne was admitted to the hospital that evening and started on a diuretic to help her shed the fluid. The change in her condition the next morning was nothing short of miraculous. By the evening of our second day at Mercy Medical Center, she had lost more than 20 pounds. The loss of fluid was more of a relief than either of us could have imagined. She was suddenly more alert, even wanting to walk around the hall. I was encouraged that the treatments seemed to be working.

Roxanne was discharged from Mercy six days later, 30 pounds lighter and feeling remarkably better. The home health nurse set up oxygen in our home and taught me how to administer the antiviral medicine in her IV. She had four chemo treatments within the next six days and they seemed to be working. Hoping that she was now on the road to recovery made me wonder how we would ever get our lives back to normal after such a life altering experience. I had put my life on hold to be with Roxanne, and I had no clue how to start over.

I felt like I had been living in a time warp for the past couple of months. The normal rhythm of my life had given way to living moment-by-moment and day-by-day. Now that Roxanne's prognosis seemed brighter, my mind was plagued with many questions. I didn't know where to turn my attention. Both my business partners really stepped up and took charge of running the office without me, but I still felt as if I had abandoned them and my responsibilities.

It was emotionally exhausting trying to determine what my next steps should be. I knew Roxanne had to be my number one priority, but the responsibility I felt toward my co-workers and clients was overwhelming. When Roxanne was feeling well, I knew she was fine with other family members taking care of her, but when she wasn't feeling well, she wanted and needed me. I wondered if I should hire someone to take care of her and go back to work part time, but I wasn't sure I could bear to leave her for that long. I knew that I would never forgive myself if something happened to her while I was working, and I didn't make it home in time.

During those days of feeling like I was barely keeping my head above water, my journaling allowed me to unload my crazy emotions and questions, trading them for God's divine peace. After our cruise out of New Orleans in September, I had started a new journal that I named "Divine Detours," having no clue how significant that name would become. I finished that journal on January 23, 2012, and began a new one that I named "The Journey." Our anticipated destination for this journey was total healing for Roxanne, but we could only live one day at a time, unsure of the perils we might face. It was as if I was in a raging tempest. I had never felt so totally dependent on God's strength, wisdom, and peace.

On February 1, when we met with Dr. Schnider before treatment, Roxanne was somewhat incoherent and feeling worse than she had in several weeks. After learning that her white blood cell count was elevated, I asked him if we were winning the battle. He answered that he didn't know, but he was concerned about fluid retention and the possibility of infection. As our appointment came to a close, Dr. Schnider asked if Roxanne would want to be resuscitated if her health worsened and her heart or her breathing stopped. Roxanne indicated that she understood the question. We responded that if she got that bad, we would not want her kept alive with life support. Surprisingly, Roxanne was not distressed by the question, but it rattled me to the core.

Struggling to keep my emotions in check, I rolled Roxanne to the treatment room and got her situated with her parents who had come to visit her. I hugged and kissed them and Roxanne, and then hurried to my car, where I bent over the steering wheel with my face buried in my arms and had a total meltdown. It was almost unbearable for me to watch her suffer, yet, I couldn't imagine living without her. When I reached the point of absolute physical and emotional exhaustion, a still, small voice whispered to me, "I am with you." Once again, God met me with the peace and strength I needed to go back inside and carry on with a smile.

The next few weeks were filled with treatments, procedures, and several more trips to the hospital. Her condition seemed to fluctuate from day to day. Anytime she felt up to it, I took her on walks, wheelchair rides, or short road trips. I was glad to be home where we were close to family because their visits helped keep her spirits up.

Early on the morning of February 16, I opened my journal in an attempt to sort out all the questions that had been running through my mind. God met me with a very compelling question, *"What if this does not turn out the way you hope?"* For the first time in 67 days, I wrestled with the very real possibility that Roxanne might not get well. The devastation I experienced over the next 120 minutes was so real and grueling that it seemed that she was already gone. Finally, I was able to prayerfully write, *God, thank you for every single day, every single moment you've given me with Roxanne. It has been wonderful. I would like 20 more years, but I will embrace your will. Your grace is sufficient for me.*

In that moment of surrender, I was able to go back to bed and sleep like a baby for another hour. Again, I woke up optimistic and ready to continue the fight. That test of my will convinced me of two things: I needed to be with Roxanne every minute that I could, and my business partners needed me completely out of their way.

My decision was confirmed when Dr. Schnider informed us that he was attempting to schedule an appointment for Roxanne with the head of oncology at Barnes in St. Louis. Dr. Staton, a leukemia specialist, would determine if Roxanne should be admitted there. Dr. Schnider's intention was to get Roxanne into remission and then send her to St. Louis where she would receive a bone marrow transplant. If she was eligible for the transplant, he expected that she would be in St. Louis for several months. Knowing that I would be with Roxanne during that period, I was prepared to tell my partners that I might never return to the business.

Ten days later, I was packing our bags as we waited to leave the hospital after a minor procedure. Inside one of the pockets, I found a book that we had received a month before from Mark Kelley, an old friend of Roxanne's who had been through leukemia and a bone marrow transplant. The short book was titled, *The Prisoner in the Third Cell,* by Gene Edwards. As Roxanne dozed off, I picked it up and began to read while we waited to be released. The book concluded with two haunting questions:

1) Will you trust a God that you do not understand?
2) Will you trust a God that does not meet your own expectations?

Once again, God was directing me to consider those two questions. Until very recently, I had fully expected that Roxanne would be healed. I reflected on the beginning of our journey when Roxanne and I had committed before God and nearly every person in our lives to trust Him no matter what the future held and to love and honor Him every step of the way. So far, I did not like what I had said, "Yes" to, but I knew that others were watching to see how I would handle this trial. My faithfulness was being tested like never before. It seemed that God was about to take me places in my walk of faith that I could never have imagined. We had come too far to answer those two questions with anything but another resounding "Yes."

Thankfully, we were met with some happy news when we returned home from the hospital. My daughter, Casey, and her team had made it home safely from Haiti. They facilitated 12 weddings and built 27 benches for the church that Roxanne had raised the money to build. The sparkle in Roxanne's eyes and the joy on her face upon hearing Casey's report was priceless.

Early on the morning of February 29, I awoke with a heavy heart. I was once again feeling torn between taking care of business and making sure that Roxanne was being taken care of. I tried to maintain contact with my co-workers and help them as much as I could with my workload. Unfortunately, I sensed that with Roxanne's condition, I was no longer truly dependable and was probably causing them more grief than necessary. I knew God was urging me to let that phase of my life go and continue forward with giving Roxanne my full attention and care. Without a doubt, the time had come for me to announce my permanent retirement from my business.

At 7 AM that morning I went to the leadership meeting at my company and informed my partners that they needed to take the business from that day forward and run it as if it were theirs, assuming I would never be back. I told them that once Roxanne was transferred to St. Louis, I would not be coming back to Arkansas without her. I could tell they were a little overwhelmed. Before I left, I prayed that God would lead them forward.

It occurred to me as I drove away from that meeting that the next day would be March 1, 2012, the exact date I had told my partners almost a year before that they needed to be able to run the company without me. I was amazed at God's grace in giving me the exact date nine months in advance. I shared that with Roxanne on our way to her appointment at the oncology clinic.

We both rejoiced that God had been preparing our families, friends, coworkers, and especially us, for this difficult journey. Had he not revealed to me that I would need to be absent by that time, the stress of abandoning my business would have been far too much for me to handle.

We were barely seated in the treatment room when Dr. Schnider walked in and got right to the point. He told us that the treatments were not working and he wanted to get Roxanne to St. Louis as soon as possible. That was only two hours after I had announced my permanent departure from my business. God's timing blew my mind once again.

While my mom and Roxanne's friend, Karen, sat with her during her treatment, I took the opportunity to take a short walk and process that news. As I was coming back up the stairs to the treatment room, Roxanne became extremely cold and began shaking violently, struggling to breathe. After a short ambulance ride to Mercy Hospital and five hours in the ER, she was back in ICU. As I collapsed into bed about midnight, all I could say was, "Wow, God, what a day."

The next few days were crazy. Dr. Schnider was trying to arrange a hospital-to-hospital transfer to Barnes. He wanted to put a semi-permanent catheter in Roxanne's right side so we could drain excess fluid from her lung daily at home without having to go to the hospital every few days. Unfortunately, she was running a fever, so they were afraid to do the surgery.

Despite the doctor's plans, Roxanne had only one thing on her mind. She desperately wanted to go to Elise's baby shower the following Saturday. She begged her nurse practitioner, Hannah, to find a way to get her out of the hospital long enough to attend the shower. Although Roxanne and I both prayed that somehow she would be able to go, I didn't see any way that could happen since she was so sick. The other problem was that Dr. Schnider wanted to get her transferred while she was still in the hospital, so I feared that he would be reluctant to release her for any reason.

On Friday morning, Dr. Bundee and Hannah concluded that

she urgently needed a catheter placed, and convinced her surgeons to put it in as soon as possible. In spite of their concerns about Roxanne's fever, she was in surgery by noon. I assumed they would keep her in the hospital to make sure that she remained in stable condition. To my surprise, she was released and we were home by 6:30 Friday evening.

Early the next morning, a home health nurse came and taught me how to empty the catheter and change the bandage around it. As the nurse drove away, Roxanne was eager to get ready for the baby shower. Miraculously, she was feeling better that day than she had in two months. She even told everyone at the shower that she felt cancer free. She spent over two hours there and had her picture taken with everyone. When I picked her up she was exhausted, but

I know she wouldn't have traded that time for anything. I was so thankful that Dr. Bundee and Hannah cared enough to relax the protocol so that she could have the chance to share another special moment with nearly all the women in our family.

On March 5, Dr. Staton from Barnes Jewish Hospital in St. Louis called to schedule an appointment for us to meet with him at his office for testing on March 15. He didn't indicate whether or not she would be admitted. I worried if Roxanne could make the six-hour trip there and back without complications. Also, Jon announced that he and his fiance' wanted to be married on March 17th, in our backyard under our wedding arch. There was a chance that Roxanne might be able to go to the wedding if she wasn't admitted to Barnes, but it would be very risky. If she were admitted, both of us would definitely miss the wedding, which broke our hearts. Regardless, I knew we would have to drive to St. Louis, not knowing the outcome and pray that Dr. Staton would know what was best for her.

Roxanne's condition declined steadily over the next week. She was constantly nauseated and getting weaker by the day. While I didn't mention it to her, I decided that there was no way I could drive her to St. Louis by myself. I was relieved when Monday finally came so that I could share my concerns with Dr. Schnider when I took her in for treatment. After examining her, he suggested that we go to the hospital right after the treatment so that she could receive a few pints of blood. He agreed that she was far too ill to travel by car and he planned to initiate a hospital-to-hospital transfer by ambulance as soon as possible.

The next few days were pretty wild. Friends and family poured into Roxanne's room when they heard that we were leaving soon for St. Louis. Roxanne tried to be gracious with each visitor, but she was quite ill and tired easily. When I could tell she was exhausted, I politely asked everyone to leave so she could rest.

Our bags were packed so that we could leave in a moment's notice. I got our home prepared for our long absence and our backyard ready for Jon's wedding. The bills were paid and I had done everything at the office that I could do. Every morning the doctor assured us that we would be transferred that day and every evening the nurse would tell us that no bed was available in St. Louis. It was a very difficult time and my journal entries expressed my frustration.

3-15-12: *Well, Lord, it's 5 AM and we're looking out the windows at the end of the hall, sitting in extremely uncomfortable chairs that we can't possibly sleep in. We slept very little tonight since Roxanne is quite sick. She woke up about 2 AM and hollered, "Help!" I sprung up off my cot just in time to see her start vomiting. She soaked her bedding and her gown. It was pretty awful. She probably made a mistake begging them to take the tube out of her nose that was keeping her stomach cleared. She can't seem to win the battle with nausea any other way. I sent an update last night asking Team Roxanne to pray that the blockage in her intestines would be cleared. Lord, that seemed like such a simple request and 70 people agreed in prayer. I thought that surely You would do it, but apparently not. Why not, Lord?? Yet, I reminded myself that I committed to trusting You when I do not understand and even when You do not meet my expectations. It's really hard to do that, Lord, when I'm tired from very little sleep, I don't understand and especially when I really do have expectations. I'm a bit grumpy when I've had no sleep and my wife wants to sit at the end of the building where I know I can't possibly sleep.*

3-17-12 - 1 AM: *Well, Lord, I am sitting down at the end of the building looking out the window with Roxanne. We are in the exact same spot where we were a couple of nights ago. I felt very frustrated about being here that night. Tonight, Roxanne is restless again. She wanted to get out of her bed and sit on the end of my pullout cot, so I helped her move over. Since I had been so grumpy last time she asked, she sheepishly said, "Babe, do you think we could go sit by the window at the end of the building again?" My first thought was that it was one o'clock in the morning. But I didn't say that. Instead, I said "Sure, Babe. If you need to go down there, we will go." As I was helping her move into that uncomfortable chair where she loved to sit and look out the window, she said to me, "Thank you, Sweetheart. Thank you so much." In that moment, my heart broke. I realized that she had been in that hospital room so long that she just needed out of that room. It's such a small thing to do, but it's extremely important to her. I am writing this so I never forget this lesson. Forgive me, Lord, when I'm selfish. I am too often.*

Suddenly, I understood what Jesus meant when He said that there is no greater love than to lay down your life for another. While God was not asking me to literally die for my wife in that instant, He was asking me to figuratively die to myself in a small way in order to comfort and care for her. I learned that, "laying down" even a moment of my life to make her smile or laugh was a precious gift that I could give her.

On our fourth day at Mercy Hospital, we were still waiting to be transferred to St. Louis. Every evening they told us that there was no bed available at Barnes, yet, every day I watched Roxanne getting sicker. Keeping my attitude in check and my eyes focused on the Lord was no easy task. Roxanne seemed to be having an easier time with it, encouraging me as often as she could. I was so proud of how strong she was. She promised that she wouldn't give up and told me she would be okay, but I still couldn't help but be worried. Trusting God had never been as difficult as it seemed then.

POINTS 2 PONDER
SACRIFICIAL love ▸ ≫

1: How would you define sacrificial love?

_____

_____

_____

_____

2: If you are in a relationship, how can you demonstrate sacrificial love to your significant other?

_____

_____

_____

_____

3: Consider the question Dr. Schnider asked Roxanne about being resuscitated if her heart and breathing stopped. How would you answer?

_____

_____

_____

_____

4: Have you discussed your wishes on this matter with those closest to you? Why, or why not?

_____

_____

_____

_____

5: Think of the person that means the most to you. Have you ever thought you might lose them? How would you react if you did? Share your thoughts and feelings:

_____

_____

_____

_____

6: Sometimes life circumstances seem to blast you in multiple ways. Describe a time like that in your life:

_____

_____

_____

_____

7: If it was in the past, describe how you were able to get through that time. If you are presently in the midst of the storm, what are you doing to get through it?

_____

_____

_____

_____

struck down but not
DESTROYED

"Live for today, but hold your hands open to tomorrow. Anticipate the future and it's changes with joy. There is a seed of God's love in every event, every unpleasant situation in which you may find yourself."

- Barbara Johnson

When we first checked into Mercy, we were sure we would not be able to attend Jon's wedding later that week. At 9:30 AM on March 17, our fifth day in the hospital, we were still waiting for a bed to open up in St. Louis so Roxanne could be transferred. Jon was scheduled to marry at 6 PM that evening. I had asked our nurse practitioner, Hannah, if there was any way I could take Roxanne on a long walk and then sneak out for the wedding. She said she would consider giving her a two-hour pass if her health would allow.

When Bobby learned that his mom might go to Jon's wedding, he shared something with me that had been on his heart for a few weeks. Realizing he might not get to dance with his mom at his own wedding, he wanted to dance with her and record it. He was hoping he might able to do that at Jon's wedding if she was able to go. The night before the wedding, I prayed five specific requests and asked Team Roxanne to join me. I requested that:

1. Roxanne would sleep through the night.
2. She would wake up feeling better the next morning.
3. We would be able to attend the wedding.
4. Bobby would get the chance to dance with his mom at the wedding.
5. A bed would open up in St. Louis shortly after the wedding.

I had high hopes that God was going to work it out for us to attend the wedding, believing that was the reason Roxanne had not yet been transferred. We just needed a little window of time where she could feel good enough to enjoy the wedding, just like God had given her for Elise's baby shower.

For some reason, God answered each of my prayer requests, "No, Son. We're not going to do it that way, but I am with you." Roxanne had a very restless night and we spent most of it sitting at the end of the hall looking out the window watching cars go by. I was torn between wanting to go to Jon's wedding and knowing we needed to get Roxanne to St. Louis in hopes of finding new treatment options.

When Hannah came on the morning of the 17th, she looked at me with watery eyes and said, "She's too sick, Roger. I can't let her go. I'm so sorry. I really hoped we could." All I could do was nod in agreement, because I knew she was right. I then sent the following text to Team Roxanne:

3-17-12 - 9 AM: *When I began sending you these text updates, I had no idea where that would take us. I gave you five prayer requests last night. For the moment, it appears that God has answered all five with "no." I don't understand and this doesn't meet my expectations, but I choose to continue to trust God. Why are you on this journey with us? I don't know for sure, but my guess is that God wants to teach you something about His ways through our journey. So, I feel compelled to share these things with you. In case you're wondering, I am writing this with tears dripping down my face. I am sharing about choosing faith, but my heart is breaking. Life can be really painful and though God allows us to walk through the pain, He does not leave us. He does not forget us and He understands our feelings. Even Jesus grieved and said, "Father, if it be possible, take this cup from Me. Yet, not My will, but Thine be done." He knew God's will was best, but even so, He had to deal with His human feelings. These setbacks and disappointments Roxanne and I have faced are not the whole story and we're still choosing to dance in the rain. I hope you catch a glimpse of God's love for all of us as we make this journey together.*

Sincerely trying to obey,

Roger

By 10 AM that morning, visitors began to pour in. Soon Roxanne's room and the waiting room were filled with family and friends. She tired out quickly, so at noon I asked everyone to leave so she could rest. At 3 PM, Roxanne's sister, Sandra, burst into the room saying, "Naomi's father is going to film the wedding on Skype, and Roxanne and I will watch it in her room. Roger, you can go to the wedding and come back."

I sat at Roxanne's bedside thinking maybe I was really going to Jon's wedding after all when a nurse suddenly walked in. She announced that a room had just opened up in St. Louis. Hoping we could leave right after the wedding, I asked the nurse to request the ambulance to pick us up at 8 PM. The nurse came back a few minutes later to report, "Unfortunately, you will have to go at 5 PM or you will lose your room." I was sick at the thought of missing the wedding by only an hour, but I had no time to dwell on that. I had to start preparing for our six-hour ambulance ride.

Just to be safe, I asked the nurse to confirm that I could ride in the ambulance with Roxanne. I didn't want them arriving in St. Louis before me. I knew that upon her arrival, the nurses at Barnes would ask Roxanne all kinds of questions that she was clearly in no shape to answer. I also knew she would feel so much better if I could be right there holding her hand on that long ride. I had requested every day for the entire week to be allowed to ride with her. I had our bags packed and even had my car parked in the garage at home so that we could leave straight from the hospital.

The nurse returned 15 minutes later to inform me that I absolutely could not ride in the ambulance. Her apologetic tone told me how hard it was for her to tell me that. I fell apart. It was 3:45 PM and they planned to pick her up at 5 PM. Frustrated and anxious, I asked Bobby and Travis to go get my car. I quickly drained the fluid off her lung. Then I tried to make sure everything was packed for the trip.

My sweet Roxanne just kept patting my arm and assuring me, "It's okay, Babe. I'm going to be just fine. It's only six hours. I will do great." It did not feel fine to me though. I felt like a piece of wallpaper that was being ripped off the wall that it had been glued to for years. Only a few moments before, I had imagined attending Jon's wedding, hurrying back to the hospital, climbing into the ambulance and comforting my wife on the difficult trip to St. Louis. Instead, I had to jump in my car just two hours before the wedding and race to St. Louis in a manic attempt to beat the ambulance.

As soon as the boys arrived with my car, I kissed and hugged Roxanne goodbye. I was trying hard not to break down again.

I didn't want to leave her upset. I told her I would be waiting for her in St. Louis, grabbed my suitcase, and hit the road. It was 4 PM when I drove off the hospital parking lot. I had a one-hour head start and didn't plan to stop for any reason.

I called Jon's cell phone to tell him I was not going to be at the wedding. For a couple of minutes, I was so emotional that I couldn't even talk. I was sobbing so hard I could barely see the road. I'd never felt so broken in my life. When I could finally speak, I told Jon how sorry I was not to be at the wedding, but I assured him that I was there in spirit. He gently tried to comfort me, telling me to take good care of Roxanne. I cried and poured out my heart to God for many miles on my way to St. Louis. I have often wondered how I even made it with such blurred vision.

Roxanne called right at 5 PM to tell me that she was in the ambulance about to leave. She again assured me that she was okay and would see me soon. Shortly after 6 PM, my niece, Tahnee, began texting me pictures of the wedding as it progressed. I found myself smiling and it almost felt like I was there. My favorite picture was of Jon and his bride reciting their vows beneath the same wedding arch that Roxanne and I and Travis and Elise had taken our vows under. Three generations of our family had been married under that arch in the past eight years.

In just five hours, I arrived in St. Louis. Barnes Jewish Hospital was massive, covering several city blocks. I whispered a prayer asking God to show me the way. Fortunately, I found a guard who pointed me towards the elevators in the leukemia unit. When I got to Roxanne's floor, the nurse informed me that I had beaten the ambulance. The nurse took me on a quick tour of the floor and then asked questions for 45 minutes until Roxanne arrived in the room shortly before midnight.

Although she was pretty miserable when she arrived, they wasted no time going to work on her. The room was full of doctors, nurses, and lab and x-ray technicians most of the night. I was impressed at how they concentrated on gathering her profile for Dr. Staton's review the next morning.

The next week was filled with procedures, chemo treatments and scary moments. I was panic stricken, when by the end of the week Roxanne was unable speak or respond. After hooking her up to an EEG machine to evaluate her brain activity, they discovered that she was having non-convulsive seizures. Shortly after they gave her antiseizure medication in her IV she was talking and laughing with her sister, Sandra, and me. The whole family was coming for the weekend, and I was worried that she would be exhausted by then, but once again God blessed her with a few good days when she needed them most.

Friday evening our family began to roll in for the weekend and Roxanne greeted them enthusiastically. Travis, Elise, and Bobby were the first to arrive, and they were shocked at how well she was doing. Travis exclaimed, "Wow, it's like I have my old mom back!"

Elise was eight months pregnant with Roxanne's first biological grandbaby, so they had a lot to talk about. Roxanne loved her seven grandchildren like no other, but she was especially excited about this little girl whose name was going to be Chrysalyn Roxanne. Travis and I took a walk while Roxanne and Elise talked about babies. Roxanne described a dream she'd been having. Elise thought it was so interesting that she typed Roxanne's words into her phone so she could remember them.

Saved on Elise's phone on **3-23-2012:** *I keep having this recurring dream about Chrysalyn. She has just a little bit of hair. Not much, just a little bit. Since I'm going to lose my hair, we can grow our hair in together!" After a brief pause she whispered, "I just want to hold her in my arms."*

Thankfully, Roxanne continued to feel well enough the next morning to enjoy having family there. With wires from the EEG machine hooked up to her head, she had fun cracking jokes about herself looking like a cable TV. It made my heart leap to see her so happy. When Casey, Buddy and the three grandkids came, she had a blast talking and laughing with them about how funny her voice sounded. She kept telling them she sounded like a weasel. I had not seen her having so much fun in a very long time.

After the EEG wires were removed, Tahnee and Debi came to visit, and gently washed and fixed Roxanne's hair. She was so glad to have those leads off of her head and was especially happy that Tahnee and Debi could help her with her hair rather than the nurses.

Shortly after lunch, Roxanne asked Buddy to gather all our family in her room. She wanted to tell us about a vision that she had a few days before. She said she saw herself totally naked, kneeling in front of an old rugged cross. As she knelt there, she realized that she had nothing left, and all that mattered was that cross.

Interestingly, Travis asked her some questions and even took notes about the vision.

This is the account of their conversation:

"Mom, what was the cross like?" asked Travis.
"Very rough, Son. Not smooth at all."
"What was the ground like around it?"
"It was bare and worn smooth. I knew many people had been there before me." Roxanne replied.
"What was the sky like?"
"Dark and cloudy, Son."

I found Travis's questions fascinating, but I found her clear and easy responses to the questions even more so. I had no question that the vision was very vivid and very real to Roxanne. The entire weekend was truly special for Roxanne and our family. After most of the kids said goodbye, Bobby and Tahnee told us they still had a few things planned for Roxanne that they wanted to do before they headed home. The first was to take her to the garden on the roof of the 8th floor. Roxanne had mentioned several times that week that she desperately wanted to see it. We loaded her up in a wheelchair and headed to the roof.

The garden was even more beautiful than we had hoped. There was a short walkway bordered by bursts of colorful spring flowers in full bloom. Two separate ponds were filled with an array of diverse fish and a bubbling waterfall created a tranquil environment. It was absolutely breathtaking.

As we rolled Roxanne back into her room Bobby said, "Mom, can we do our dance now?" Roxanne responded, "You're going to have to hold me up, Son. I'm not strong enough to stand." Bobby had recorded, "The Perfect Fan" by the Backstreet Boys on his phone, the same song that was played when Travis danced with her at his wedding. The lyrics are a beautiful tribute to how both boys felt about their mom.

Bobby started the music and gently picked his mom up in his arms. He held her full weight and swayed to the music for the entire song. I could barely see the giant smile on her face through my tears. That moment will now be one of my most treasured memories. I've never been more proud of Bobby than I was in that moment. I knew it meant the world to Roxanne as well. Tahnee recorded it on video so that Bobby can someday share his dance with his mom at his wedding. I couldn't have been happier that they had that special moment together.

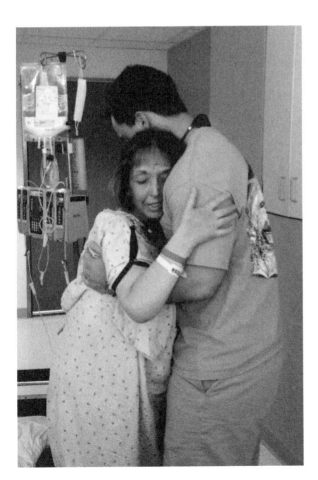

Roxanne later texted Bobby, *"Today was a highlight of my life when we danced. Thanks for everything. I love you so much."* As I settled Roxanne into her bed for the night, her eyes sparkled as she told me that was one of the best weekends of her life. I could tell she was exhausted and slipping back into her sickness, but I was so thankful that God had blessed her with such an incredible time with her family.

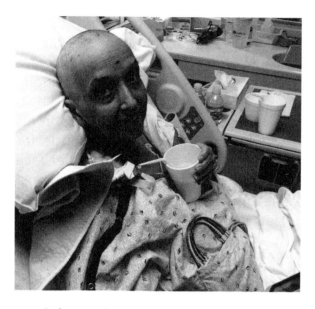

I awoke at 4 AM the next morning to the sound of women cackling and hair clippers buzzing. Roxanne hadn't told me, but she had decided to shave her head before her hair fell out. One of the nurses even volunteered to do it for her. They seemed to be having way too much fun with it. However, I was encouraged that no matter how bad things were, she always found something to laugh about.

Joining in on the fun, I walked over and told my newly bald wife that she still looked hot. Travis and Bobby both decided to shave their heads the same day to show their support, which made her feel extra special. Later that morning, Roxanne said, "Babe, last night God really spoke to me. He said just a little longer and the suffering will be over." I could tell she was happy about that message and it had given her peace.

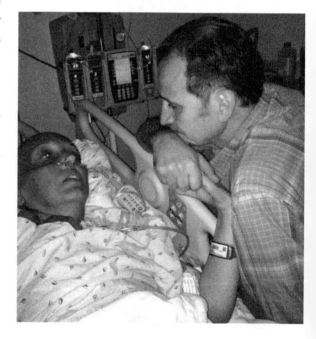

Clasping her hand tightly, I shuddered at

the thought of what it could mean: either she would start getting better, or she would soon pass away. I tried my best to stay positive, but it was all I could do not to cry. Choosing to believe that she was going to get better, I told her I was excited about that.

For the first time in my life and in our marriage, I felt like some of my fears and what the doctors and nurses shared with me I needed to carry alone, and not burden Roxanne with.

The next three weeks were extremely busy and tough. There were several days when Roxanne struggled so much that she seemed like a totally different person. Instead of sharing the often gruesome and unpleasant details, I am going to give you this leg of the story the same way Team Roxanne got it.

Text to Team Roxanne **March 28, 2012:** *Good morning. Last night was a very rough night. Roxanne was in a lot of pain yesterday. Our dear friends, Ray and Judi, were here from California. She enjoyed them so much. This journey has been long and I confess that we're exhausted, but praise God for friends, family, and remarkable doctors and nurses whose encouragement makes it tolerable. God's amazing grace keeps us going. The little cleaning lady who mops the floors and dumps the trash each day has encouraged my heart so much. She just loves Jesus, prays for the patients and serves the Lord right where He put her in a quiet, humble way. That is a picture of true Christianity. Not greatness, just humble obedience. I am awed by her faithfulness. We need God's grace to finish this journey. Roxanne's sisters did their blood tests to see if one of them was a match for the bone marrow transplant. Dr. Staton said she has to be a lot healthier before we can begin the procedure. That defines our prayer request for today. On this journey, may we be as faithful as our cleaning lady.*

Text to Team Roxanne **March 30, 2012:** *It's been a good day. Once more we need to pray that the blockage in her intestines will clear. It is silly what you find yourself praying for when you live in a hospital. But, for her, this is actually very critical. Thanks for your prayers.*

Text to Team Roxanne **March 31, 2012:**

Lessons from the hospital:

1. Real love is a choice and calls for sacrifice.
2. Your true friends surface when life gets tough.
3. You can, in fact, do all things through Christ who strengthens you.
4. Nursing is an amazing ministry.
5. It really is the little things that matter most.
6. Giving is more rewarding than receiving.
7. Life is very uncertain, so don't leave things unsaid.
8. God is there and He is trustworthy even when we don't understand His ways.
10. Answered prayer does not always look the way we want it to.

Text to Team Roxanne **April 2, 2012:** *I have learned something about myself the last couple of days. I'm trying my best to trust God even when things don't make sense. What I realized today was that, as I honestly try to trust Him, I develop new expectations for what God should or will do if I'm faithful. In essence, I put new expectations on the situation. God answered our prayer for clearing the blockage. Yet, once again, I find myself saying, "God, I expected everything to be much better, but instead it's worse." So, the journey continues. Please pray for Roxanne's overall health. She has to be much healthier and stronger for them to do a successful bone marrow transplant. Pray that one of her sisters is a match. And pray that we won't get discouraged when we don't understand why bad things are happening and they don't go the way we want. Pray that we will trust God and stay the course. Love y'all, Roger.*

Text to Team Roxanne **April 4, 2012:** *The prayer request today is very simple. We need a serious upturn in Roxanne's overall health. She is due for round two of chemo, but the doctors are concerned that she's not strong enough to handle it. She's sleeping very little. She needs a serious touch from the Master. Please pray that we get that very soon.*

Text to Team Roxanne **April 5, 2012:** *How do I update the last 24 hours? It's been a crazy roller coaster. Last night at 10:30, we were the first to see our new granddaughter live on Skype just moments after she was born. This morning Roxanne is struggling to breathe. Our friends, Gail and Sheila, came from Branson to visit, but Roxanne could hardly acknowledge that they were there. They took her to radiology to pull the fluid off her lungs again, but she passed out before they could do the procedure. They raced her back to her room and got her oxygen saturation level back up. Then the hospitalist came in and said, "Mrs. Clement, I can do this procedure for you here in your room. Do you think you can you sit up so I can do it?" She simply shook her head. I told the doctor, "Let's do it. I can hold her up." I held her carefully in my arms as he inserted the needle to remove the fluid. I could feel her breathing improve as he extracted several liters. She fell asleep as I fought back tears of relief. For a guy who has never cried much, I find all sorts of reasons to do it now. As I tried to regain my composure, Roxanne's sister, Sandra, called to tell me that she was a bone marrow match. After the hair-raising experience we just made it through, it was as if God was saying, "Don't worry Son, I've got this." I have to admit that I don't like all the twists and turns in this 117-day journey, but I am more confident than ever that God has everything in His hands.*

Text to Team Roxanne **April 10, 2012:** *Good morning. Roxanne is resting. I'm here alone, reflecting on the past few months. Four months ago today this journey began. Amazingly, God began preparing us an entire year before we knew Roxanne was sick. He prepared me to be able to leave my business and for my partners to take it over. God knew and moved before we had a clue. I would never have believed that I could let my business go and live in a hospital room for so long. I have to believe that God has a plan and all this is preparation for that plan. Today I am excited about what lies ahead. Thanks for your prayers and support.*

On April 13, Tiffany and two of her friends came to visit Roxanne. They arrived late in the evening but stopped by to say hello before heading to their hotel for the night. I sensed that Tiffany was a little anxious. The next morning she called to let us know that she was taking her friends to the St. Louis Zoo. They planned to come visit us afterwards. I found that a bit strange since Roxanne's condition was more concerning than ever, and they had driven 7 hours to visit her. I knew it would be hard for Tiffany to see her mom in such a weakened state, but I worried that she would have some serious regrets if she didn't spend all the quality time she could with her. Hoping to spare her such regrets, I decided to have a heart-to-heart talk with her when she got to the hospital.

When she arrived I pulled her aside and told her that I could tell she was struggling. As I spoke, tears began streaming down her cheeks. "I'm so afraid," she said. "It's too hard to see her like this. I don't want my last memories of her to be so painful."

"Tiff, this could be the last time you have with her. I know this is hard, but you will have huge regrets if you don't say everything you want to say to her. Don't let this opportunity slip by. Spend some alone time with her today. I will take your friends to lunch so you can talk."

She agreed and gave me a hug. I took her friends out for some Mexican cuisine, and we were gone for several hours. When we walked back into the hospital room, Tiffany was laying in the hospital bed with her arms wrapped around Roxanne. They had talked until they fell sound asleep. A wave of relief washed over me and I knew Tiffany would always be grateful that she had that time with her mom.

God gave Roxanne another couple of really good days the following week when her parents came to see her. There was something important that she needed to discuss with her father and she hoped to get a chance to do that during their visit. When they arrived, she had less pain, less retained fluid, and was clear-headed. They had an amazing visit and I think both of them felt a lot of peace afterward.

To keep her spirits high, I put a picture of Chrysalyn up on her

wall and told her that was one big reason to get better. My biggest concern was that her cancer would come roaring back like it did two weeks after her treatment. I prayed desperately that it wouldn't.

However, Roxanne began to go downhill rapidly in the following days. A spinal tap revealed that the cancer had spread into her central nervous system. Now we would have to fight the cancer both in her blood and in her central nervous system. If we lost the battle on either front, the likelihood of her survival would decrease exponentially. My heart sank as the hope of her healing seemed to evaporate within me. I spent some time talking to the Lord about my fears and decided to write about it.

Text to Team Roxanne **April 17, 2012:** *This is the first day I have really had to deal with the possibility that the outcome of this journey might not be what I want. I know God's grace will be sufficient, but I've cried a lot of tears today. Roxanne doesn't know anybody and hasn't opened her eyes for the last several hours. The doctor said if the treatment works in her spinal fluid, she'll probably return to a normal mental state. If not, there isn't much left to do except keep her comfortable. I had a serious talk with the doctor about just taking her home to be with her family. He wants me to wait until Thursday to see if the treatment has decreased the number of cancer cells in the spinal fluid. If it has, he thinks we should keep on fighting. If not, taking her home might be the right thing to do.*

Text to Team Roxanne **April 18, 2012:** *Roxanne never opened her eyes today. Her breathing seems a bit labored and we could not awaken her. Tomorrow we will know what the counts look like in the spinal fluid and will make a decision whether to take her home or stay the course in the hospital. Please pray that the right choice will be clear and everyone will be in agreement. They put a drain tube in her left lung today, so if we do go home we can drain the fluid there. These are hard decisions and difficult times, but God is still in control.*

POINTS2PONDER
DEALING with disappointments ▸ ≫

1: Describe something you've prayed for diligently that never happened. How did you respond to God saying, "no?"

_____

_____

_____

_____

2: Describe a time when a something bad happened. Did that experience make you run to God or from Him and why?

_____

_____

_____

_____

3: Describe a time God said, "wait" or "no" which He later used to do something even greater than you had prayed for:

_____

_____

_____

_____

17 ▶▶

stepping into
HEAVEN

"No one wants to die. Even people who want to go to heaven don't want to die to get there. And yet death is the destination we all share. No one has ever escaped it. And that is as it should be, because Death is very likely the single best invention of Life. It is Life's change agent. It clears the old to make way for the new."

- Steve Jobs

In the early morning of April 19, Roxanne had another serious breathing crisis. The room quickly filled with doctors and nurses attempting to stabilize her respirations. They managed to calm her down, but her breaths were still labored. She remained unresponsive, as she had been for the last couple of days.

Roxanne's oncologist came in and said, "I told you that I would let you know when I thought there was nothing else we could do. We have done all we can. She will probably live for only a few more hours. You don't have time to take her home." In shock and disbelief, I tried to hold myself together. I thought I had accepted the idea that she might not make it, but no one is ever truly ready to hear those words.

I quickly called the kids and told them that the oncologist had confirmed our worst fears. Knowing the likelihood of her passing away before they could arrive, I suggested that each one of them would have to make their own decision about whether to make the six-hour drive.

Our oldest son, Travis, and his wife, Elise, decided to take the risk and make the trip with their two-week-old baby Chrysalyn. Roxanne had been too ill to see her first grandchild, except in photographs and on Skype. It broke my heart to know she might never have the joy of holding baby Chrysalyn in her arms.

Our two youngest, Bobby and Tiffany, chose not to make the drive. Stepping back into the room, I bent down and whispered in Roxanne's ear, "Babe, your grandbaby is on her way. She will be here in six hours." To my surprise, her labored breathing ceased and she drifted off into a peaceful sleep. Her parents, sisters, Casey, and Buddy were all there. Astonished at how calmly she was resting, I told them, "She must be waiting for her grandbaby to get here."

The previous day, Roxanne's nurse had explained to me that hearing is the last thing to go. She said that even though a patient is unresponsive, they often still hear everything that's going on. It was Roxanne's 45th birthday and she had received more than 100 birthday cards.

I spent that day reading the cards to her aloud, confidant that she could hear me. I truly believed Roxanne heard me say, "Your grandbaby's on the way," and she was going to hold on until she got to see her.

Roxanne rested comfortably for the next six hours. At about 4 PM, Travis and Elise sent me a text saying that they were in the parking garage. I told everyone in the room, "They are here and should be in the room in about five minutes." To my shock and awe, as soon as I said that, Roxanne slowly began opening her eyes. We all waited, silently hoping the baby would make it up to the room in time. Chrysalyn got very fussy and began to cry as they rode the elevator up to our floor. By the time the baby rolled into the room in her stroller, Roxanne's eyes were fully open for the first time in three days.

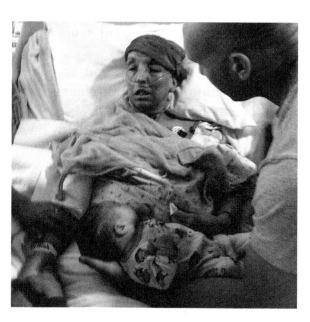

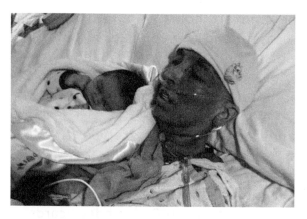

Chrysalyn immediately stopped crying, as if she somehow knew the sacredness of that moment. With all the strength she had left, Roxanne reached out as much as she could. Chrysalyn was then carefully placed into her arms. She had made it. Roxanne's eyes remained open for the next hour as she gazed down at her beautiful granddaughter. That miracle hour is forever etched in the hearts and minds of each person who witnessed it.

Shortly thereafter, Roxanne began to get restless. Travis gently picked Chrysalyn back up. I asked the nurse to give her something for pain. Roxanne went back to sleep, but her breathing soon became labored and shallow once again. We sat by her bed, taking turns holding her hand.

Several times I whispered in her ear, "Babe, I love you with all my heart. You have made me the happiest man in the world. If Jesus is calling, you go and watch for me at the gate. I love you more than anything. Thank you for being the world's greatest wife. I love you." I knew that those were the last moments I would spend with my wife, my partner, my best friend. The last few hours she just gasped a breath about every 30 seconds. So many times I thought she was not going to take another, but then she would gasp again. It was painful to watch, yet, I could not leave her.

Finally, there were no more gasps. From the moment she took her last breath, I felt a part of myself pass on with her. I knew that moment would change my life forever. Roxanne died at 10:38 PM with Casey, Buddy, Travis, Elise, Chrysalyn, and me in the room with her. I sent out a simple text message to Team Roxanne stating, *"Roxanne just stepped into heaven."*

My heart shattered. The most important and precious thing in my life had been ripped away from me. I had no clue what lay ahead. I had put all my other priorities on hold to take care of her and she was now gone. For the past eight years, we had spent every moment we could together. It didn't matter to us if we soaked in the hot tub for two hours, sat in bed watching bull riding, or walked the trails in Bella Vista, we just wanted to be together. We held hands until our fingers cramped just because we loved to be touching. I could not fathom life without her.

Filling out the hospital paperwork, I knew I wouldn't be able to sleep that night. The kids and I began packing our things and decided to make the six hour drive back home. Buddy rode with me. I told him hospital stories, describing some special moments Roxanne and I had the last few weeks. I shared my fear of crawling into bed when I got home and realizing she would never again join me there. He expressed how broken-hearted Jarvis, Carson, and Riley were going to be when they heard the news that their beloved grandma was gone.

As I dropped Buddy off in Neosho and traveled home, I reflected on the months before Roxanne was admitted to the hospital. Just two weeks before she went into the hospital in December, Roxanne and I had gone to see the movie, *Courageous*. A scene from that movie kept replaying in my mind. After his 8-year-old daughter died, the father asked his pastor to help him make sense of it all. The pastor said, "The most important decision you have to make is will you praise God for the eight years you had with her or will you be mad at God for the years you thought you should have had?" I had already answered that question months before. I again praised God for the eight amazing years I had with Roxanne. I wished I could have had many more, but I cherished what God allowed me to have. Because I never allowed myself to believe she might not make it until the last couple of days, the end came so quickly. I realized that I had been totally unprepared for that outcome.

The next few days were a whirlwind of activity as we made the arrangements for the visitation and funeral service. Travis, Bobby and I went to the funeral home early the next morning to choose a casket and discuss the funeral plan. Travis picked out the clothes she would wear, and Bobby offered to write the obituary and fax it over. Those were depressing tasks. I was glad to have them behind me and appreciated the boys for going with me. I took the boys to the cemetery to show them where she would be buried.

While we were there I told them the story of how we came to have burial plots. A couple of years before, Roxanne asked me out of the clear blue where we were going to be buried. I thought it a strange question coming from a lady 17 years younger than me.

I answered that I had no clue. I had honestly never thought about it. She explained with determination, "We need to decide and get those arrangements in place. I want to be buried beside you. I don't want anyone to ever be able to mess with that. I don't care if one of us dies tomorrow and remarries. I want us to be buried together." She was so insistent about it that I talked with my mom who had purchased four plots next to where my grandparents were buried. She buried my father there when he passed away. I bought the two extras plots from her and that made Roxanne very happy. Little did I know how much peace that decision would later provide.

The family gathered at our house to plan the service with our pastor, Mickey. Many caring friends stopped by our home with food. We talked about celebrating her life, her ministry at home and in Haiti, and her amazing family. Bobby wanted to deliver the eulogy. We told stories about Roxanne, laughed, and cried together. Although we knew there would be many tears, we truly wanted to celebrate her remarkable life. I woke up on Sunday, the day of visitation, feeling very anxious. I was almost scared about going to view Roxanne's body at the funeral home at 10 AM. I sent another text to Team Roxanne asking for their prayers. Although I hesitated to send it, my fears vanished as soon as I hit the send button.

Text to Team Roxanne **April 22, 2012:**
What does it feel like when you have lost the person you love the most?

1) Like someone has ripped your heart out and thrown it on the floor.
2) You cannot breathe or catch your breath.
3) Your nose is pressed up against the wall and you have no clue what to do.
4) The rest of your life is a fog that you're afraid to enter.
5) You are alone even in a crowd.
6) You wish you had hugged, kissed, and told them, "I love you," one more time.
7) You know they are in heaven, but being left here feels like hell.

Deep down, I know that what I feel is not a lack of faith or trust or hope. It is just what I feel and that is really okay. I wish someone had shared that with me before now, so I am sharing it with you. Have a good day.

As our family arrived at the funeral home and I saw Roxanne's body for the first time, it was apparent that it was just her shell. Her spirit was gone and with the Lord. My fears melted away, and I knew that God's grace would see me through this. Many of our family members told stories about Roxanne. My grandson, Jon, tearfully shared how very much he loved her. I told about how she hated it when I kissed her on the nose. Then, I bent down and kissed her on the nose.

More than a thousand people attended the viewing that afternoon. It was a huge testimony to the many lives Roxanne had touched. Friends came from as far away as Michigan and Illinois. One by one they told me how much she had impacted their lives. I was simply overwhelmed by how radically this sweet, soft-spoken country girl had changed her world. I was blessed by this outpouring of love and support for Roxanne and our family.

On the way to the funeral the next day, Tiffany asked me a question that rocked my world. "You are still going to walk me down the aisle, right?" She was afraid that since Roxanne had gone that I, too, might fade out of her life. I suddenly understood why I could not go back to work and bury my sorrows in busy work. Roxanne's three kids needed to know that I was still there for them and that my presence in their lives would always be important to me. They needed to know that even though Roxanne was gone, I was still going to be their dad.

Earlier that morning, Roxanne's good friend, Sue, had sent me a text concerning the kids that said, "Lead them with Roxanne's heart - sweet, tender, gentle, listening, and generous." What sage advice. That very moment I committed to being proactive in helping them through the grieving process. I assured them that they would never be alone. I knew that Roxanne's shoes would be hard to fill, but I also knew that I had to try.

The funeral was truly amazing. A huge crowd gathered in the auditorium once again. Mickey did a beautiful job of presenting the gospel using Roxanne's love and sincerity as a role model. Our youngest son, Bobby, moved us to tears as he described how his mother had been an incredible woman as well as a loving, giving, and wise mother. He also told of how Roxanne and I had provided a picture for him and his siblings of what a marriage should look like and how to do it right. He gave a beautiful tribute for a beautiful lady.

A few other family members shared some fond memories. Then the microphone was passed to anyone who had a story to tell about how Roxanne had impacted their life. Several shared how different their lives would have been without her and the blessings she had brought their way. As the funeral came to a close, Mickey sang, "Thank You" by Ray Boltz. Photographs of Roxanne with the many people whose lives she had touched flashed across the screen on center stage. The smiles on the faces of the Haitian children as she embraced them showed how they were truly blessed by her giving.

While it was astounding to see how many lives she had changed through giving her time, money and abounding love, I realized that the life she had changed the most was mine. She gave me the happiest eight years of my life and taught me how to truly enjoy life. She was my constant source of joy from the moment I met her until the moment she took her last breath. Because of her tender, patient heart toward the Lord even in the midst of her suffering, I could not dare be angry with God. He had not answered my prayers for healing the way I hoped, but He kept a smile on her face, which put a smile on mine. He gave us some of the most precious moments of our lives in the last months before she faded into glory. Though my heart was broken, it also overflowed with thankfulness that God was making Himself very noticeably present.

The emptiness began to settle in after the funeral was over and everyone headed back home. For the first time, the sharp reality of being alone hit me like a ton of bricks. Her passing would change my life even more in the future since I had already told my partners that I would not be coming back to my business, which had been my livelihood and ministry for the past 22 years. Deep down I wondered, *"What do I do now, Lord?"*

POINTS 2 PONDER
SACRIFICIAL love ▸ ≫

1: What do you want people to say about you after you're gone?

_____

_____

_____

_____

2: What are you doing to make sure you live up to what you want people to say about you after you're gone?

_____

_____

_____

_____

3: Are you confident that if you died today you would step into heaven? Why or why not?

_____

_____

_____

_____

4: Are you confident that all the people you love will go to heaven when they die? If not, what can you do to show them the love of Christ?

_____

_____

_____

_____

_____

_____

_____

18 ⟫

valley of
GRIEF

"Don't ever discount the wonder of your tears. They can be healing waters and a stream of joy. Sometimes they are the best words the heart can speak."

- William Paul Young , *The Shack*

Grief has a way of stripping you down to your real, vulnerable self. Jesus was described as a man "acquainted with grief." Strangely enough, I was almost 62 years old before I had a clue what grief really meant. I had experienced loss and sadness in my life when I lost my father, my grandparents, and a special uncle, but nothing compared to the agony of losing a spouse. In each of those situations, I shed a few tears, was sad for a few days, and was aware of their absence. In retrospect however, I realized that life quickly returned to normal.

The loss of Roxanne, however, seared my soul. As the waves of grief crashed and battered me, I discovered things inside me that I never knew existed. I now have a depth of compassion, understanding and connection with others that I've never experienced before. I found myself in a foreign place - the deepest valley of grief I had ever known. I felt like a tetherball, cut off from its pole and tossed into an angry sea with no bearing as to where I was. I did the only thing I knew to do and cried out to God in my journal.

4-21-12: *Good morning, Lord. I woke up this morning with the horrible realization that I'm never going to see Roxanne again. She is never going to show up. I am not going to wake up with her beside me. This isn't a dream, it's a nightmare. She is not coming back. There is an ache inside that I cannot explain. I wonder what more I could have done. Did I tell her I loved her enough? Could I have held her more? Oh, Lord, this is a pain I have never experienced. I am going to miss her so badly. I sit here thinking, I wish I would have rubbed her feet more, held her more and climbed over the tubes and laid in that hospital bed with her more. I wish I could tell her I love her a few more times, take her on one more trip, or just sit and look into those pretty green eyes for a few more hours. However, I want to thank You for eight amazing years.*

4-23-12: *Today, we bury Roxanne. This marks the end of a long and life-changing battle that began December 10, 2011. The visitation yesterday was amazing. The outpouring of love was remarkable. What will life be like* *after today? I do not know. What will I do when the funeral is over and everyone is gone? I trust You, Lord. I know You will lead me. I want to make good choices—help me.*

Before losing Roxanne, I had always been a self-confident, self-disciplined and stable kind of guy, but now, I find myself insecure and emotionally out of control on a regular basis, and often with no forewarning. The emotional turmoil I've experienced has had more side effects than I ever imagined. For instance, my memory has nearly evaporated. I can see people I have known for years and be unable to recall their first name. In the past, I prided myself on my ability to focus, which gave me an advantage when helping others with financial and personal matters. I'm not sure where my memory went, but my ability to concentrate apparently went with it. I've had a hard time focusing on the simplest of tasks. I had always been convinced that I could overcome anything if I set my mind to it, but trying to tame my heartache seems as impossible as trying to tame a dog with rabies. At first, crying sessions became frequent and could side swipe me at any random moment. This level of anguish I've experienced makes maintaining my masculine and "put together" image nearly impossible. A few days after the funeral, I walked into my house, glanced at a picture of Roxanne and me and began to sob uncontrollably. The emotional outburst caught me completely off guard. It was as if the handle broke off of a water faucet with the water still running and I was helpless to stop the flow.

The sobbing eventually turned into wailing. That also took me by surprise. The wailing usually came when I had finally grown accustomed to my sobbing sessions. I would suddenly feel something in the pit of my stomach moving up my body, through my chest and out my mouth as a very loud groan, scream or a sound I can't even describe. I had no idea I was capable of such a response. You might be thinking, "Wow, Roger, those first few weeks must've been really rough." I assure you they were, but at that point I had barely even scratched the surface of my sorrow. Almost 11 months later, I was driving on the old bike route that Roxanne and I used to ride down nearly every evening. As I reminisced about past rides, I began to cry and wail so intensely that I had to pull the car over twice to regain my composure.

When I first started these uncontrollable crying and sobbing sessions, I was profoundly uncomfortable. I would be angry and disappointed at myself for letting my feelings get the best of me. However, I've come to see the value of allowing visible demonstrations of my angst. When I was young I was almost afraid to cry, thinking it made me appear weak. I realize now, that being able to cry openly has made me a stronger, more real and open person. Healing is taking place inside me. To my surprise the expression of my personal pain gives friends and family permission to express their pain as well. I am experiencing deeper, more authentic relationships as a result.

I attended an amazing 15-week program called Grief Share. The second session of our weekly class, we tell our personal stories of loss and pass around a picture of our loved one. Initially that was intimidating. Before long though, hearing each person's story established a common bond among us. At our first meeting, we are all strangers, but by the end of week two, we are more like soldiers headed together into the battle of grief. This close-knit group who could relate to my situation became a powerful tool in my healing process.

One of the various aspects of grief discussed in the weekly videos was that of being "ambushed" by grief. That is a great description of what happens when you're least expecting it. A song, a smell, a picture, or just a mental flashback can overwhelm and crash over you like a tidal wave.

You may be wondering what happened to that "peace that passes all understanding" I have talked so much about. Thankfully, I am still experiencing it. God has never left me. My confidence that I will see Roxanne again has never wavered. I often wonder how a person who has no hope in God could make it through such a loss. Unfortunately, my faith does not spare me from the pain that grief brings. Somewhat like open-heart surgery, grief is extremely invasive and is followed by a very long and painful recovery process. With no shortcuts to healing, I am just along for the ride and hoping for a full recovery. Another thing I learned in one of my Grief Share sessions was that if I tried to circumvent the natural grieving process and move on too quickly, grief will resurface later and be even more severe and difficult to deal with. That concept made more sense when I heard a sermon by Rick Warren after the loss of his son. He commented that, "If I don't let it out in a healthy way, then I'll act it out in an unhealthy way." I realized that the same was true for myself. Each time I tried to bury my sorrow, if even for a few moments, I could feel the tension rising beyond my ability to deal with it. Each time I let my feelings out, a wave of relief washed over me and I felt ready to face the day again. I promised myself that I would never try to take the easy way out, but rather walk through my sorrow with courage and be better for it.

I confess that I had previously been totally ignorant of how to help others who were grieving, but as I journeyed through my own grief, I saw others and myself in a whole new light. Looking back before my loss, I remembered one of my longtime friends and employees who lost her husband a few years ago. When she noticed that I was stumbling around trying to figure out what to say to her, she graciously gave me some guidance through a post she had printed from an internet website for widows. I found it to be so helpful that I am sharing it with you. I wish someone had given it to me long ago.

How Can You Help Me?

Please talk about my loved one, even though he's gone. It is more comforting to cry than pretend he never existed. I need to talk about him and I need to do it over and over.

Please be patient with me. Nothing feels secure in my world. Get comfortable with my crying. Sadness hits me in waves and I never know when my tears may flow. Just sit with me in silence and hold my hand.

Don't abandon me with the excuse that you don't want to upset me. You can't catch my grief. My world is painful and when you are too afraid to call me, visit, or say anything, you isolate me at a time when I most need to be cared about.

If you don't know what to say, just come over, give me a hug or touch my arm and gently say, "I'm sorry." You can even say, "I just don't know what to say, but I care and I want you to know that."

Just because I look good does not mean I feel good. Ask me how I feel only if you really have time to find out.

I will never totally recover. This is not a cold or the flu. I'm not sick. I'm grieving and that's much different. Don't think I will be over it in a year. For I am not only grieving his death, but also the person I was when I was with him, the life that we shared, the plans we had for watching our children and our grandchildren grow, the places we will never get to go together, and the hopes and dreams that will never come true. My whole world is crumbled and I will never be the same.

I will not always be grieving as intensely, but I will never forget my loved one and rather than recover, I want to incorporate his life and love into the rest of my life. He is a part of me and always will be. Sometimes I will remember him with joy, other times with a tear. Both are okay.

I don't have to accept the death. Yes, I have to understand that it has happened and it is real, but there are some things in life that are just not acceptable.

When you tell me what I should be doing, I feel even more lost and alone. I feel badly enough that my loved one is dead, so please don't make it worse by telling me I'm not doing this right.

Please don't tell me I can find someone else or that I need to start dating again. I'm not ready and I may never be. Besides, what makes you think people are replaceable? They aren't. Whoever comes after will always be someone different.

I don't even understand what you mean when you say,

"You've got to get on with your life." My life is going on. I've been forced to take on new responsibilities and roles. It may not look the way you think it should. This will take time and I will never be my old self again. So please, just love me as I am today, and know that with your love and support, the joy will return slowly to my life. But I will never forget and there will always be times that I cry.

I need to know that you care about me. I need to feel your touch, your hugs. I need you just to be with me and I need to be with you. I need to know you believe in me and in my ability to get through my grief in my own way and in my own time.

Please don't say, *"Call me if you need anything."* I'll never call you because I have no idea what I need. Trying to figure out what you could do for me takes more energy than I have. So, in advance, let me give you some ideas:

Bring food or a movie over we can watch together.

Send me a card on special holidays, his birthday, and the anniversary of his death, and be sure to mention his name. You can't make me cry. The tears are here and I will love you for giving me the opportunity to shed them because someone cared enough about me to reach out on a difficult day.

Ask me more than once to join you at a movie, lunch, or dinner. I may say no at first or even for a while, but please don't give up on me because somewhere down the road, I may be ready and if you've given up, then I will really be alone.

Understand how difficult it is for me to be surrounded by couples, to walk into events alone, to go home alone, and to feel out of place in the same situations where I used to feel so comfortable.

Please don't judge me now or think I'm behaving strangely. Remember I'm grieving. I may even be in shock. I am afraid. I may feel deep rage. I may even feel guilty. But above all, I am hurt. I am experiencing a pain unlike any I've ever felt before and one that can't be imagined by anyone who has not walked in my shoes.

Don't worry if you think I'm getting better and then suddenly I seem to slip backward. Grief makes me behave this way at times.

Please don't tell me you know how I feel or that it's time to get on with my life. What I need is a time to grieve.

Most of all, thank you for being my friend. Thank you for your patience. Thank you for caring. Thank you for helping and understanding. Thank you for praying for me.

Remember in the days or years ahead, after your loss—when you need me as I have needed you—I will understand. And then I will come and be with you.

- Author Unknown

That passage opened my eyes to the wide range of emotions, actions and reactions one can expect from a person in mourning. Ashamed of how I had failed employees, family members and friends in the past, I resolved to be much more sensitive in the future.

The similarities between being single after my divorce and following the death of my spouse proved to be oddly similar. It was a very unwelcome déjà vu. After comparing those two periods in my life, I realized that there are some valuable observations I could learn from. Here are some of the most common responses I received during both of those periods in my life:

1. Most people, including close friends and family members, often avoided me, either because they didn't know how to respond, they simply didn't want to deal with it, or they were just afraid to talk about it.

2. I felt that some people judged whether I was "healing" properly or by acceptable methods. They even tried to categorize my emotional state and insinuate that I was not trying hard enough to move on.

3. I noticed that in both cases, when I tried to have a personal or hypothetical conversation about death or divorce, it made others noticeably uncomfortable, so they often sent unspoken messages to change the subject and avoid the realities implied. Sadly, this applied to friends and family. Even my church family, from whom I had hoped to find encouragement and comfort.

During both periods of solitude in my life, I was forced to deal with the painful realities that my loss brought. I was shocked at the pain I experienced due to the lack of understanding and care shown by those I expected it from most. Regretfully, those realities put me in a very vulnerable position. As a result of the unconcerned response I received from most people, my fear of loneliness and sense of abandonment became overwhelming. I could tell that my risk of getting into an unhealthy relationship or resorting to unhealthy habits increased exponentially as my loneliness and grief increased. The more poorly others responded to me, the more needy I felt for a relationship. The good news is that God never forsook me. In fact, He often sent a friend, a church member, or an acquaintance that proved to be a lifesaver when I needed it most. Still, I found myself discovering the truth about grief primarily on my own.

As the anniversary of Roxanne's passing approached, I could feel the tension mounting up within me. I found myself struggling to stay focused and motivated, much like I did at my previous job shortly before we learned that Roxanne was ill. The reality that an entire year had gone by made the finality of her death more vivid than ever to me.

As I considered different options on what I should do to celebrate Roxanne's life on the anniversary of her passing, I decided to plan a drop-in gathering. Friends and family could come by and share stories, eat snacks and write a note to Roxanne for her birthday. Her 46th birthday would be the day before the anniversary of her death. I was surprised that some family and friends didn't seem too excited about the idea, but I felt it was a necessary step in my healing process.

The drop in turned out to be a great success. We had a sweet time of sharing and nearly everyone who came wrote a little note to Roxanne and tied it to a helium filled balloon. At the end of the evening we released 46 balloons representing what would have been her 46th year. Even baby Chrysalyn let one go. We watched our notes slowly ascending into the heavens and imagined Roxanne's spirit rising to meet God in the same way.

Accepting death as a real and normal part of life is really hard for most people. The reality is that no one lives forever. If we embrace that truth, it changes a number of things. Our relationship with God becomes a central question to deal with rather than something to ignore and put off until a more convenient time. How we treat others also becomes vitally important. Some of the saddest stories I heard in Grief Share were from people who were at odds with their loved one when he or she died. The guilt and shame they felt compounded their grief exponentially. Words can't express how thankful I am that I was spared

from such heavy regrets. If you realize that every encounter with another person could be your last, it will change the way you relate to people, your priorities and what you believe is important. Had I not treated every moment with Roxanne as if it might be my last, I might be permanently stuck in the guilt I would feel from not having spent more time with her. It is essential that we learn how to deal with death in a healthy way. We need to hold onto this life lightly, because it doesn't last. The best time to think about eternity is now because we will all face it sooner than we think.

POINTS 2 PONDER
HOPE in the valley ▸ ❯❯

1: Why do you think people often avoid the subject of death?

_____

_____

_____

_____

2: Why do you think people avoid those who are hurting or grieving?

_____

_____

_____

_____

3: How would you feel if you lost a loved one or experienced some other tragedy and your friends avoided or ignored you rather than helped you get through it?

_____

_____

_____

_____

4: Name someone in your life who is hurting. What things can you do or say to help or encourage that person?

_____

_____

_____

_____

_____

_____

5: Why do you think it would be hurtful to tell someone to get over it and move on?

_____

_____

_____

_____

healing through
HELPING

"We are all wounded. But wounds are necessary for His healing light to enter into our beings. Without wounds and failure and frustrations and defeats, there will be no opening for His brilliance to trickle in and invade our lives."

- Bo Sanchez

have been blessed to witness the full extent of Roxanne's ministry on an ongoing basis, which has inspired and challenged me to the core. After Roxanne's death, my daughter, Casey, took over her share of responsibilities for the mission team, both in the States and in Haiti. Casey now trains new mission teams, visiting Haiti as often as possible. One day she called to check on me and asked if I would consider going with them on their next trip. Roxanne and I had planned to go together in January, 2012, but after she passed away, I laid my plans to visit Haiti to rest. However, while talking to Casey, the thought crossed my mind that perhaps God still wanted me to go, and if it was His plan, I wanted to be willing.

As Casey shared about the possibility of me joining the next mission team, she told me that The Jesus Church of Santos specifically requested that I come, because they wanted to have a special service in Roxanne's honor. Before Roxanne got sick, Norma from JoyHouse had asked her to name the schoolroom being built beneath the church's sanctuary, since the room was originally her idea. She named it, "The Promise Room," based on the promise in Philippians 1:6, "Being confident of this, that He who began a good work in you will carry it to completion until the day of Christ Jesus." The room had been completed, but they were holding off the dedication service with hopes that I could attend.

Because of her hard work raising the money to rebuild their sanctuary, Roxanne clearly held a special place in the hearts of the congregation there. It touched my heart that they wanted me to be there to see the dedication ceremony and that they were even willing to postpone it for me. I knew it was an invitation that would be hard to pass up.

Although I had never planned to go to Haiti after Roxanne's death, as I considered the possibility, I became curious about why she was so dedicated to her ministry there. I also realized that visiting the people she loved so much might be a healing experience I might later regret missing. After praying about it for a few days, I signed up, completely convinced that God was leading me to go, but I was so nervous that it was difficult to get excited about the trip.

I had hoped that my anxiety would turn to excitement by the time I boarded my flight to Haiti, but that was not the case. I was apprehensive as the plane descended and the rusty tin roofs of Port-au-Prince came into view. A wave of emotions washed over me: fear, anxiety, sadness, dread, exhilaration, and hopeful anticipation all rolled into one powerful surge. My head and heart reeled from such a mixture of emotions all at once. My thoughts turned to Joe, one of the founders of JoyHouse, and Pastor Eddie, who were meeting me at the airport. Roxanne had shared so much about Pastor Eddie that I felt like I knew him.

Like many other Haitian men who worked with JoyHouse, Eddie had lived in an orphanage until Norma and Joe rescued him. He now served as pastor of The Jesus Church of Santos that Roxanne worked hard to rebuild, and he had also officiated The Joyful Weddings that Roxanne coordinated. Because of the kindness he had shown to Roxanne and the love she had for him, I worried that I might throw my arms around him and weep hysterically as soon as I met him. In an attempt to distract myself, I tried to imagine the excitement Roxanne must have felt the first time she landed in Port-au-Prince. As I looked out the window, I caught a glimpse of the country that had captured her heart when she was only 8-years-old.

As Joe, Pastor Eddie and I made our way to JoyHouse in their 1960's bus, I found myself unable to talk or even look at them for fear that the floodgates restraining my grief would open and I would never stop weeping. I wanted to tell him about Roxanne's illness and death, to thank him for his loving kindness toward her, and to share how much she had loved and appreciated him. Fortunately, the activity in the streets slowly diverted my attention.

As we turned onto the steep rocky road leading to the JoyHouse gate, I noticed a number of men walking toward the church, each hauling what appeared to be two large bags of trash. Upon arrival, I greeted Norma and my daughter, Casey, picked a bunk in the men's dorm room, and hurried down to the church to learn more about what was going on.

The mission project for that morning was to give the men of the area an opportunity to work and earn some money by picking up trash. After they entered the church, the mission team discarded their trash and visited with them through an interpreter. I smiled when I saw the last man arrive. He was old and toothless, but he grinned from ear to ear, obviously proud of what he had accomplished in collecting his bags of trash. The team then shared the gospel with each of them and handed them each a five-dollar bill and a Creole New Testament.

Later that afternoon, the mission team walked through a community near JoyHouse. The majority of families in that neighborhood lived in the hundreds of 10 x 12 foot plywood houses which had been built after the earthquake by the Samaritan's Purse ministry. Our interpreter pointed out that several families were still using the temporary houses that Roxanne had helped to assemble. Most of the tiny houses had no running water, electricity, bathroom facilities, or windows, but I soon learned that those people felt very privileged to have a roof over their heads.

The next morning we stacked plastic tubs filled with diapers, wipes, vitamins, and other medical supplies into JoyHouse's old white truck. The team loaded into the back of the truck to ride the four miles to the church. The last half-mile was up a steep hill on a very rough road. Each time the truck hit a rut, we all laughed hysterically as we bounced high into the air.

The church was like an open pavilion with a tin roof. The rough benches were already full of mothers and their babies awaiting our arrival. Our project, referred to as the Daniel Project, was to address the nutritional needs of mothers and their babies. A registered nurse examined the babies, then discussed health issues and specific nutritional recommendations with the mothers. Many Haitian babies were malnourished because their mothers couldn't produce milk, nor could they afford to buy milk. Some resorted to feeding them whatever they could find, including the water they used to boil rice.

The mission team's nurse gave the mothers vitamins, medicine, and other medical supplies to help them in caring for their babies. The mothers and their children came dressed in their Sunday best, clothing donations that had come in after the earthquake. A toddler in a pretty white dress stood beside me, a wet spot growing on the ground beneath her feet. It took me a moment to realize that she had no diaper, so her urine simply ran down her leg. As I was trying to wrap my mind around that, I saw another mother holding her baby while a dark spot was forming on her dress. I was stunned by the awareness that most of those mothers could not afford diapers, therefore they just did without. We gave each mother a bag of diapers and wipes, but I wished that we could give each one a whole case. I tried to imagine how it must have felt to be a mother, unable to provide milk or diapers for my children to keep them healthy and clean. It broke my heart.

My job was to pray, through an interpreter, for each of the mothers and their children before they left. Humbled by their gentle and grateful spirits, when I asked them how I could pray for them, I expected answers related to their basic needs. Instead, I repeatedly got the same two answers, "Pray that I will grow spiritually," and "Pray that God will supply the money for our children to go to school." I suddenly understood why Roxanne was so passionate about the church starting a school for the local children, and was honored that they were dedicating the schoolroom to her.

The team was quiet in the back of the truck as we made the trip back to JoyHouse. Our thoughts were consumed by the sobering reality of how hard Haitian life is and how immense their needs are. Once again, I found myself thanking God for things I had often taken for granted such as the free school system in America, and that I always had diapers for my babies.

That evening, the dedication service was held for the schoolroom beneath church. Amazed at how many Haitians walked for miles just to attend the service, I wondered how many people I knew back home who would be willing to walk several miles to church if they didn't have a vehicle.

Norma opened the meeting by sharing that after the earthquake flattened the original church, they had put up a makeshift tent to use for a place of worship. She told the story of Roxanne's first trip to Haiti and her commitment to go home and raise the money to rebuild the church. Norma went on to say that many people had made promises to help over the years that she had been at JoyHouse, but few had ever followed through. Roxanne, however, went home and did precisely what she had promised to do.

Norma happily reported that the student population had grown from an initial seven students to 56. As I heard that testimony, I knew that Roxanne would be absolutely thrilled to know that her hard work was still paying off and that many children would get the opportunity for an education and the ability to provide better lives for themselves and their families. During the service, I told the story of how at 8 years old, Roxanne donated her camp money to a Haiti missionary and for the next 33 years she remained determined to help the people of Haiti. I told everyone that it reminded me that God's plan doesn't always unfold quickly, but it does unfold in His time. In that bittersweet moment, I cried tears of sorrow for my loss, mingled with tears of joy for the Haitians that had and would be blessed by her sacrifice.

The next morning was December 2, 2012. I sat on the roof of JoyHouse in the same spot where Roxanne had her morning devotion on her first trip to Haiti. Sipping my instant coffee, I looked out over the rooftops at the deep blue ocean. The warm breeze fanning my face filled my nostrils with the mixed scents of salt, barnyard, and trash. Were it not for the crowing of the rooster and the gusts of odor permeating my nostrils, I would swear the ocean view I beheld was that of a paradise island.

Reaching for my journal, I flipped through the pages until I got to December 2, 2011, exactly one year before. My heart stopped short, my throat started to close up and I struggled to catch my breath as I began to read what had transpired exactly a year ago. I realized that it was 6 AM on December 2, 2011, when Roxanne and I had sat on our couch and prayed together, committing to say, "Yes" to God's plan for our lives even if we didn't like it. Eight days after that prayer, I took her to the emergency room and the most difficult journey of our lives began.

As I reflected on the past year, I had to be honest with the Lord and say, *"Lord, I know You're at work, I know You're with me, I know You have a plan to help many others, and I am thankful. Even so, I must tell you I haven't liked this plan very much. I have never hurt so badly in my life. The ache in my heart never stops. I will miss her terribly the rest of my life."* Sitting there looking out over Haiti with tears in my eyes, God seemed to say, *"I know, Son, now what are you going to do this year?"* Pondering for a moment, I wrote, *"I will still say, "Yes" to your plans for this next year, Lord, even if I don't like them."* It was frightening to imagine what that would entail, or what else God might ask of me, but I was willing.

Later that morning, I was shocked to enter the church and

find it packed with standing room only. Tears of joy flooded my eyes as I realized that the church could hold twice as many people as the tent in which Roxanne had worshipped. I cried through most of the service as I listened to familiar hymns sung in Creole and watched the kids from The Promise Room school file in and sit together. My broken heart swelled with pride as I saw how many people had been affected by Roxanne's life. To my surprise and delight, I saw that same old Haitian man with no teeth kneel at the altar and invite Jesus to be his Savior. He then turned and smiled as if he had just entered the gates of heaven and was gazing upon his heavenly family for the first time. He practically strutted back to his seat.

The mission team and the JoyHouse staff sat on the roof that evening for a time of fellowship. We opened with a few praise songs in both Creole and English. Afterwards, Roland, who was the first boy that Norma and Joe rescued from the orphanage, shared his incredible testimony. I was deeply moved. He came from a poor family with eight children, and when he was very young, his parents took him and his sister to the orphanage because they couldn't feed them all. Someone in America, whom he never met, sent $15 a month so that he could be fed and clothed. He was incredibly thankful for the unknown person who had provided for him. I was in awe of how much a commitment of only $15 a month could radically change the life of another person.

After our worship time, another JoyHouse staff member named Gerald shared that he and his wife were one of the first couples to be married during the Joyful Weddings project. He said, "Because of Roxanne, I had a wedding that was more beautiful than I ever could've hoped for." I was ashamed as I remembered how I had grumbled under my breath when I had to haul five heavy suitcases into the airport for Roxanne to take to Haiti for the weddings. I now saw what a tremendous gift that had been to this precious couple. I was astounded by the power of giving in what once seemed like such an insignificant way.

Lying in my bed that night, I buried my face in my pillow and cried tears I no longer knew how to explain. Were they tears of sorrow because I missed the love of my life? Or were they tears of joy for becoming aware of how many lives Roxanne had positively altered? The one thing I knew for sure was that I would return home a different person.

I had agreed to go to Haiti primarily out of curiosity, yet I now realize that my time there was an extraordinary time of healing. Everyone who had known Roxanne blessed me with their stories about her trips there. Seeing the smiling faces of those Haitian children in the school dedicated to her memory was priceless. It occurred to me then that I might never have seen them if she had recovered. Losing her seemed like the most awful thing that could have ever happened to me, but in comparison with what many of those Haitians had endured, I have led an astonishingly easy and blessed life.

For the first time, I fully understood why the Bible stresses the importance of loving and helping others who are less fortunate than we are. It is because doing so positively impacts both the giver and the receiver. Praying and worshiping with the Haitian people was a healing experience like no other. Though the months after Roxanne's death seemed long and difficult, seeing the humility and love for Christ in the eyes of the Haitian people was a precious gift to me. It gave me a new perspective, allowing me to see the full extent of God's blessings in my life. My heart overflowed with thankfulness like never before.

Casey and me on the roof of JoyHouse

1: How has God used other people in your life to bless you financially, spiritually or emotionally?

_____

_____

_____

_____

2: How have you experienced healing through caring for others?

_____

_____

_____

_____

3: If you had to live in a 10 x 12 foot home with no electricity or water, how would that make you feel and why?

_____

_____

_____

_____

4: How would you define necessity?

_____

_____

_____

_____

_____

5: How does your definition of necessity differ from that of the Haitians?

_____

_____

_____

_____

redeeming
CHOICES

"The root of all difficulties is a lack of the sense of the presence of God."

- Emmett Fox

Reprioritizing my life and learning to be alone again has been incredibly difficult. Even in the midst of my grief, I sensed a divine call toward another purpose. As you can see by these journal entries shortly after Roxanne's funeral, even then, God was pulling me into a new calling.

4-24-2012: *Good morning, Lord. That moment has arrived. The funeral is over and everyone has gone home. Four and a half months in the hospital, one week of preparing and it's all over. My partners have the letter of intent ready and I told them to move forward with it. I've seen Your hand in this whole journey thus far, so where do I go from here? What do I do now? I don't want to make any mistakes, get busy or just do what's easiest. I want to know Your plan for me and follow it. God, I don't want to spend the rest of my life being self-centered. I want to share, encourage, help and develop those I love. Help me, Lord.*

4-27-12: *I feel very weird when I am alone, Lord. I guess I just have to learn to do this. I feel like one of the reasons I can't go back to work is the kids. They have lost their mom and they don't need to lose me also due to work. I need to give them a sense of stability. It's still so hard to imagine that she's gone. That thought rips my heart out. Wow, Lord! You just gave me the verse, Hebrews 12:12-13: "So take a new grip with your tired hands and stand firm on your shaky legs. Mark a straight path for your feet. Then those who follow you, though they are weak and lame, will not stumble and fall, but will become strong." God, help me mark out a straight path for my feet. Let me lead others to You in the days that I have left.*

Several members of Team Roxanne stayed in contact with me after God called Roxanne home. They shared how our journey had impacted their lives and suggested that I write a book. My first thought was, I can't even write a good paper, much less a book. But every time it was suggested, the stirring in my heart intensified and my courage grew.

Several times I told God that I wasn't skilled enough, smart enough, strong enough or brave enough, but that did not relieve my conviction. Finally, the call was overwhelming. I simply could do nothing else. Less than three weeks after the funeral, I began writing Divine Detours, and I must admit I had no idea what I signed up for.

The writing process quickly evolved into a spiritual boot camp, bringing me to a deeper level of understanding of the principles Roxanne and I lived by. It has been one of the most difficult, time consuming, heart wrenching and frustrating tasks I have ever attempted. It took all the courage I could muster to relive the moments I have shared with you in the pages of this book.

I have been more vulnerable publicly than I ever planned to be, risking criticism and even ridicule. Yet, God has provided for it in a big way by sending me several skilled helpers and encouragers. He has revealed Himself more clearly through this process than I ever could have imagined, and made my faith stronger than ever. He has taken me places I never expected and taught me valuable lessons that will help me remain strong for the journey that lies ahead.

I now believe that the story of Roxanne's life will inspire people to live in the power of love, free from the tyranny of fear, loss and death. I also have faith that my reports of God's faithfulness can motivate people to want to know Him and bring hope to anyone experiencing personal tragedy. If telling our story will make a difference in the life of one person, then the suffering I have experienced in this process will have been well worth the cost.

Though the valley of grief has been long, and my healing is slow, no sadness could steal the joy I have found in watching God work on me. No one could ever replace Roxanne, and I will always feel that loss. But with Christ, my heart has grown and softened. Where I was once mostly callous and selfish, I've seen God replacing it with tenderness and love. Where I once was driven by fear, I'm experiencing a new found courage. My eyes are opening. I see things I never saw before, and am capable of feeling them deeper than I ever have. I feel as if I am waking up from a very long sleep. My sense of purpose grows stronger day by day, and Roxanne's life continues to inspire me to try harder, to love deeper, and to take the time to care for other people.

Perhaps you are wondering, "How can a person experience such a devastating loss and not be angry at God?" or, at least, "How can you not be depressed after losing the love of your life?" The answer may surprise you. Without a doubt, my response to the tragedy of losing my spouse was years in the making. While I know I can't control every circumstance, I've learned I can control my attitude, what I choose to focus on, and my responses even in my darkest moments.

God has given us this amazing promise in Romans 8:28, "And we know that in all things, God works for the good of those who love Him, who have been called according to His purpose." As we know, not all things in this world are good. People do bad things and bad things happen to good people. The promise of the verse for believers is not that God will only give us good things, but that He can take even the terrible things that happen in our lives and ultimately bring good out of them.   Because of that promise, we can apply I Thessalonians 5:18, which reads:"Give thanks in all circumstances, for this is God's will for you in Christ Jesus." I first began learning the value of that principle shortly after I gave my life to Christ. Realizing God wants us to praise Him in all circumstances, even the negative ones, I started out with small things, such as smashing my thumb or having a minor car accident. Then, as my faith grew, it became easier to praise Him even in the most difficult and often heart breaking situations.

> **▸》God didn't promise me health, wealth and happiness. He did promise joy, peace and His continued presence in my pain.**

I can go to Him for peace, comfort and direction, because I know that God did not promise me health, wealth and happiness. He did promise joy, peace and His continued presence in my pain. That is a promise He has definitely kept. When our journey seemed to be at it's lowest point, He always let me know that He was with me whispering an encouraging word. He often sent a friend, or at times a complete stranger, to lift my spirits and give me hope. There were even moments when I felt His hand on my shoulder, reminding me that I was not alone.

Through every choice I made during Roxanne's numerous hospitalizations, God brought me into a deeper revelation of Himself. Before the journey even began, my loving Heavenly Father offered me a choice, "Will you accept my plan for your life even if you don't like it?" I now realize that He didn't have to ask me that. An all-powerful, all-knowing God does not need to ask my permission to act, nor does He act based on my feelings. Why, then, does He ask at all? The answer is because He loves me. He has a greater purpose for me than I know, but the choice is still mine. I can only discover that destiny when I choose to accept His love for me and His plan for my life.

Only God knows the mountains and valleys that I will encounter. Only He understands that no matter how heavy the burdens I bear, they will be lighter simply because I choose to accept them as being filtered through His loving hands. Making the choice to accept any path He led me down actually transformed my fear to peace, my failures to His glories, and my pain to His praise. That seemingly simple choice gave me peace in the present, and hope for the future, even in the face of death itself. It is a peace and hope that simply defy explanation.

It is that same peace and hope that has driven me to share our story with you, giving you a glimpse of how the love of God really works. It does not work to prevent hardship, but it softens the blow of each passing storm and gives us the strength to keep going when it seems that all is lost. Today my life would be very different if I had not chosen to make redeeming choices on a daily basis. Had I been fearful, angry, and bitter throughout the last months of Roxanne's life, I would have more pain in my heart now than I could bear. God's unfailing mercy spared me from the deepest pain of all, regret.

Every day I am challenged to ask myself this question, "What will I do with the lemons I have been handed?" That is really the most important question I must answer. I knew turning inward and withdrawing from the world would likely make me a bitter recluse. If I choose to dwell on the unfairness of losing the love of my life, I would easily waste the potential I have been given to help others. By sharing my story, I can testify the faithfulness of God, the power and peace of His presence and the truth of His word. I have been given numerous opportunities to encourage and minister to the sick, as well as family and friends who have lost loved ones since Roxanne's passing. I believe many more opportunities will come in the days ahead.

I could write a fairly lengthy book filled with stories of disappointments, failures, problems and heartache. My dad died when I was 24, Tiffany wrecked her first car, Roxanne had to get braces, Bobby had to have two shoulder surgeries, Travis hit a deer in his Jeep and, in retaliation, a herd of deer ate Roxanne's flowers. The list goes on and on. Life is an adventure in dealing with complications. However, God promises that if we trust Him, He will ultimately work those things out for our good. He has the amazing ability to turn obstacles into opportunities for growth, learning, improving and maturing.

None of us are exempt from suffering, though we would like to be. Losing Roxanne was undoubtedly the most painful experience of my life, but I knew that being resentful and bitter would not help me or anyone else feel better.

In the midst of her pain, Roxanne never spent one moment questioning God or being angry with Him. In fact, the first thing she told us when the diagnosis was confirmed was, "Don't be mad at God for this." She understood that successful living is not about the good things that happen to us, the victories we win, the fame we achieve, or the riches we gather. It is about what we do when life does not go our way. When her life took an unexpected turn, her true character broke through. Both Roxanne and I made the decision to trust God from the beginning. That is why she never said, "This isn't fair," or asked the question, "Why me?" Without hesitation, she simply accepted the position she found herself in and decided to use her lemons to make lemonade.

With a smile on her face, she spent the majority of her time in the hospital encouraging others and pointing them to the Lord. She never let pain or fear of death spoil her outlook or destroy her trust in God. Because of her powerful example, not a soul who witnessed it could be disillusioned with God. Instead, we were overwhelmed with thankfulness for His presence and awestruck by His power in her life.

I can do no less than to continue to praise His name, follow His lead, and trust that He has a divine plan for the rest of my life. By sharing my story with you, I hope your heart is encouraged to know that God is real, He is ever present, and He loves you. He can provide what you need right when you need it. He can give you grace, peace, wisdom and answers, even when it seems impossible. If we keep our trust in Him, He can bring something good out of every difficult or painful situation we face.

In short, making lemonade is a process, and God took me through it step by step .

POINTS 2 PONDER
LEMONS to lemonade »»

1: Describe the worst thing that has ever happened to you in your life. How did you come to terms and deal with it?

_____

_____

_____

_____

2: When something horrible happens, our first reaction can be very telling. In the situation you described above, what was your initial reaction? (fear, faith, anger, disbelief, prayer?) What did you learn about yourself through that experience?

_____

_____

_____

_____

3: Describe an occasion you perceived as a tragedy that eventually proved to be a blessing in your life.

_____

_____

_____

_____

4: How can you show God that you trust Him in your loss?

_____

_____

_____

_____

5: If you were going to lose everything in your life, but could choose to keep one thing, what would you choose to keep?

_____

_____

_____

_____

finishing
STRONG

"Courage, to me, is doing something daring, no matter how afraid, insecure, intimidated, alone, unworthy, incapable, ridiculed, or whatever paralyzing emotion you might feel. Courage is taking action... No matter what. So you're afraid? Be afraid. Be scared silly to the point you're trembling and nauseous, but do it anyway!"

- Richelle E. Goodrich, *Smile Anyway*

Before cancer rocked my world, my concept of finishing strong in life was the American Dream - an easy, comfortable retirement where I could enjoy the fruits of my labor without worry. As I approached retirement age, I planned to work less and spend more time with Roxanne, traveling as long as our health would permit. I worked hard so that we would have the financial means to do whatever we wanted during our golden years.

Today my concept of finishing strong has been radically altered. As I have labored through the process of writing this book I have gained fresh perspective and have grown immensely through my grief. I have come to recognize that my past desires for comfort had lulled me into complacency. Unaware that comfort had slowly stifled my courage, I often put on a brave face, but deep down I was afraid of change, challenge, risk, or anything outside of what I had planned for. I was trapped in my comfort zone.

It was an eye opener for me to realize that I had been motivated by fear in many areas of my life. Because of the increasing instability of the market, I worried about not having enough retirement funds, not owning a reliable and well-insured vehicle, and not having medical and life insurance policies, and even about protecting my business from economic distress.

Consequently, I had a plan in place for every possible market shift and a financial nest egg to shelter me from any future discomfort. Just the things a professional in finance would consider. Unfortunately, I was trusting in my own ability to provide far more than I was relying upon God.

In addition to what I now call my "protection planning," I also had an extensive mental list of "nevers," which I told myself I preferred not do, for one reason or another. These things didn't fit in my vision for myself, and most of them seemed impractical. I would never go back into ministry, never write a book, and definitely never visit homeless, needy, or incarcerated people. I would never pick up a hitchhiker or stop to help someone with a broken down vehicle, because that didn't seem very safe. I certainly never thought I would go to Haiti, especially without Roxanne. As it turns out, my preferences were really just fears that I didn't want to acknowledge.

As of today, I have done nearly everything on my "never" list. God has consistently presented me with unexpected and often uncomfortable opportunities to overcome the fears that have kept me from ministering to people in specific situations. Each time I have confronted a fear, I have become a little braver and a little stronger. I could literally write another book about the challenges and growth opportunities I have experienced during the writing of this book and my journey towards fearlessness, but instead, I would like to share a few of the most miraculous experiences with you.

For instance, the thought of visiting a jail used to terrify me. That may sound silly, but just the thought of going there made my heart race. As if the concertina wired fences weren't intimidating enough, I simply didn't know how to encourage someone who was behind bars. Even if I did, I was sure they wouldn't care to listen. I had never felt called to visit anyone in particular, so I was perfectly content to avoid jails altogether.

That was, until I got a phone call informing me that a young woman named Cindy, whom I knew quite well, had been arrested for obstruction of justice while trying to protect her boyfriend. I immediately knew the Lord wanted me to visit her. I also learned that her boyfriend, Jake, had been arrested as well, but for different reasons.

Jake, whom I had met only once, had a lonely and troubled past. When he found out that he and Cindy would not be able to make rent and would possibly become homeless, he panicked. Overcome by fear, he made a decision that will most likely affect the rest of his life, he decided to rob a convenience store. He had no idea that a single decision based on fear would drastically alter the course of his life, and Cindy's.

At first I fought the idea of visiting Cindy because I wasn't sure what to say or do that might help. However, the Lord simply wouldn't let me put it off for long. I knew in my heart that I needed to go. Finally, I relented and made an appointment to see her. My heart raced as I walked past the barbed wire fences toward the office where I had to sign in. Even checking in was unnerving. But then, as I sat on the other side of the glass window, phone in hand, my heart broke. My fear melted away and my only concern was how to encourage her as much as I could. I struggled to find the right words to say, but as we parted I promised that I would visit again.

After several visits it became apparent that she was more concerned about Jake than she was about herself. "Do you think you could go and see my boyfriend, too?" she asked shyly. "He really doesn't have anyone," she explained, "I am really worried about him."

Suddenly the fear that had subsided came roaring back. But before I could give the excuse that I barely knew him and that He probably wouldn't want to see me anyway, I heard that still small voice say, "You must face this fear, too." A little reluctantly, I told her that I would visit him as well and make sure he was okay. Tears streamed down her face as I prayed for her before I left.

It took me two whole weeks to finally get an appointment with Jake. When I walked in and sat down I could tell he was confused that a nearly complete stranger had come to visit him. As I sat down, tears began streaming down his face. "I'm so sorry for this," he said. "I know it's my fault Cindy is in jail right now. I'm so sorry." I could tell he was sincere. My heart softened toward him, and over the next hour, we got to know each other a bit. He opened up to me the way people used to with Roxanne, and I was shocked. Although I was initially unsure of how to respond, I told him that God loved him and had a plan and purpose for his life right where he was in spite of the mistakes he had made. We said goodbye and I promised him I would visit him again soon.

As I walked out, I began to cry. I wondered how God could show Himself mighty in such a place, to a young man so full of hurt and with such little hope. Then I began to pray, *Lord reveal Yourself to Jake. Manifest yourself to Him and change His life forever. Show him how much You love him, and give him strength to make it through these hard times.*

The following week I went to visit Jake again, his smile lit up the room. He looked like a different person. When I picked up the phone, he began pouring out his heart to me again. He told me that he had accepted Jesus as his Savior and he was more at peace than he had ever been before. When he said, "Jesus is here with me," my heart nearly burst with joy.

A few weeks later, I tried to go see Jake but the jail was not allowing visitors due to weather conditions. I was torn up inside that he would have no visitors the week of Christmas. After all my family festivities were over, I made an appointment to visit Jake again just a few days after Christmas. I was expecting him to be upset, disappointed, or even grumpy that he had to spend his holiday in jail.

Instead, the first words out of his mouth were, "I just had the best Christmas of my life! I got a Christmas card from a total stranger. It made my day and she even put some money in my account for treats. I made Christmas cards for several inmates too. They loved them. I told them all about how Jesus has touched my life."

Around the same time, Cindy shared with me that she had accepted Christ as well. I could tell she was different immediately. Seven months after our first meeting, she was released. She now has a steady job, is involved in church, and regularly shares her newfound faith with nearly everyone she meets.

Though Jake is still serving his time, he has now started a personal jail ministry by sharing about the healing and hope he has found in Christ through a Celebrate Recovery workbook. Celebrate Recovery, or CR, is a safe place for people of all walks of life who struggle with hurts of all kinds, and celebrate God's healing love as it mends their broken lives. Though he has never had the opportunity to attend a meeting, I had given him the CR material to read during one of my visits.

During one of my more recent visits, I met the mother of one of his cellmates. She shared how much of a positive impact Jake has been on her son. Though Jake only had one copy of a Celebrate Recovery workbook, he had hand written several more to pass out to his friends, and her son was one of the recipients. Overjoyed to see how God has been working in his life and using his story to bring hope and peace to others, Jake has truly experienced the power of redeeming choices.

Looking back, I realized that Cindy and Jake might have never come to the Lord if I had ignored the Holy Spirit and allowed fear to paralyze me rather than facing it for the cause of love. It made me wonder how many times I have missed the opportunity to witness changed lives because I let fear hold me back.

God gave me another opportunity to overcome fear and witness transformation through the CR program. Initially I had planned to go in support of a friend, but God had other plans. The evening we were scheduled to attend, my friend had an emergency situation and was unable to go with me. Even though he canceled, I felt a tug in my heart urging me to go. I have probably never been more scared and uncomfortable in my life. *What do these people think of me being here?* I wondered. *Are they judging me? Do they think I have the same problems as they do?*

I made it through the service but the anxiety lingered. When my friend wanted to go to CR the following week, I had a strong desire to bail. I asked God to help me go for his sake and to have peace about it. Once I set foot in the auditorium, my fear subsided. I was deeply touched by the honest, heart wrenching testimony that was shared. After the group service, my friend and I went to an orientation about the Open Share Groups that are an important part of the CR experience.

As we joined the smaller group setting, fear crept up on me again and I tried to think of a reason to leave. Amazingly, as each man told his life story and described his inner struggles, God gave me an overwhelming sense of peace and a divine love for each person

》**The openness I once feared was really a doorway for forgiveness, healing and freedom.**

in the group. I was captivated by their stories and inspired by their honesty and transparency.

As I listened, it was obvious to me that the openness I had once feared was really a doorway for forgiveness, healing and freedom. CR had opened my eyes to God's active love, acceptance and forgiveness in the world today. The freedom I found in that circle of struggling believers and truth-seekers was incredible. More importantly, I better understand the unique example of Jesus who loved and valued others even in their sin. By choosing to love someone regardless of their struggles, we are demonstrating faith in that person, as well as in God's ability to work within that person's heart. That level of acceptance inspires and challenges people to rise above their circumstances and their sin, and to keep fighting for a better way of life.

Now more than ever, I understand the miracle of love that Roxanne brought to my life. She was a precious model of Christ's love. She was fearless long before me, but I praise God for the two year journey that brought me here. That's what made her an incredible person and I understand a little better why I had to write this book and share our story.

We all have a choice to live each day with purpose and to seek the Lord in every season of life. You may find yourself on a different path than you had envisioned for yourself, but don't let fear take the wheel. As I have surrendered my fear and dared to love fully, the detours in my life have become pathways to peace, growth and unexpected blessings. While you will certainly experience some divine detours of your own, dare to make a lasting impact on those you love and those God will bring across your path as you travel the road He has laid out for you.

POINTS2PONDER
TRADING COMFORT for courage

1: What does finishing strong look like to you?

_____

_____

_____

_____

2: 1 John 4:18 says that "there is no fear in love" and that "perfect love drives out fear." Describe a time when fear seemed to hold you back and you pushed beyond it to demonstrate love:

_____

_____

_____

_____

3: Are you willing to love even when it does not make sense and requires great sacrifice? Why or why not?

_____

_____

_____

_____

4: Describe an instance where a painful detour became a platform for growth and a source of unexpected blessings:

_____

_____

_____

_____

_____

_____

5: Are you on what seems to be a detour right now? Describe it:

_____

_____

_____

_____

6: What is the benefit of saying, "Yes," to God's plan for your life in the midst of unhappy circumstances?

_____

_____

_____

_____

 THANKS

Thank you so much for taking the time to walk through this "detour" with me. I truly hope that your life has been blessed from the discoveries God has revealed to me throughout this experience.

If you are in the midst of a detour yourself, please know that I believe God had you in mind when He tasked me with the quest to pen this journey.

These past two years, God has given me the grace to share with you the depth of my sorrow over the loss of my love, Roxanne. As I have labored through this, my thoughts and prayers have been with you, my fellow travelers. Whatever detour you find yourself taking, I am confident of what our God can do in and through the lives of those who are willing to seek and obey The One who deserves our hearts.

I want to encourage you to "live out loud" by sharing your journey whenever and wherever you can. Not only will it help you, it may be just the thing a friend, loved one, or even stranger needs to hear to encourage them on their journey down life's highway.

ENDNOTES

01 ›› Wilson, Sandra (2001) Hurt People Hurt People,
Grand Rapids, MI: Discovery House Publishers

› Nouwen, Henri (1999) The Only Necessary Thing,
New York, NY: Crossroads Publishing Co.

02 ›› Weldern, Charles (1999) Christian Ethics Today,
(25:26),p.18 "If it feels good, do it!",www.christianethicstoday.com

› New Civil Society The Challenge Before Us,
September 01, 2011

03 ›› American Psychological Association,
www.apa.org/topics/divorce
Fox News Magazine
www.magazine.foxnews.com/love/whats-divorce-rate

› Chapman, Gary (1995) The Five Love Languages,
Chicago, IL: Moody Publishers

› Harley, William F. (2001) Fall In Love, Stay In Love
Grand Rapids, MI: Fleming H. Revell, a division of Baker Publishing Group

07 ›› Phillipians 4:19, **NIV**

09 ›› Psalm 56:3, **NIV**

11 ›› Hillman,Os- (2000, November 29) A Heavenly Strategic
Planning Session, In The Workplace, TGIF, (v.1)
www.intheworkplace.com

ENDNOTES

12 ›› *Anderson, Mac & Gallagher, B.J.* (2009)
Learning To Dance In The Rain,
Naperville, IL: Simple Truths, a division of Source Books, Inc.
Psalm 62:5-6, **NKJV**

14 ›› *2 Chronicles 20:12b, 15b, 17a,* **NKJV**

15 ›› *Edwards, Gene* (1991) *The Prisoner In The Third Cell,*
Carol Stream, IL: Tyndale House Publishers, Inc.
John 11:1-44, **NKJV**

18 ›› *Romans 8:28,* **NKJV**

19 ›› *Widow's Voice, Blogspot* (2012) *How Can
You Help Me?, Widow's Voice,* Soaring Spirits Loss Foundation
http://widowsvoice-sslf.blogspot.com/2012/12/how-you-can-help.html

Scripture Verses:

NIV Life Application Bible,
Zondervan {A part of Harper Collins Christian Publishing } (Copyright 2011)
Grand Rapids, MI

NKJV, Thomas Nelson Publishers, (Copyright 1975) Grand Rapids, MI

CPSIA information can be obtained at www.ICGtesting.com
Printed in the USA
BVOW11s1322091114

374176BV00001B/1/P